REBEL

A Guide for Controlling Outcomes and Defining Your Future

Carlton Robert Collins

Published in the United States by Carlton Robert Collins, Founder of EDUC8theWORLD, LLC, Cincinnati, Ohio, USA.

ISBN: 978-1-365-57588-4

Printed in the United States of America on acid-free paper

www.EDUC8theWORLD.org

(For all wholesale purchasing and copyright permission requests, reach the publisher via website listed above.)

Book Art Designed by Logan Douglas

Table of Contents

* 44 has had tremendous significance in my life and on our society. This is an acknowledgement of how a person can live in complete opposition to what people believed that he could accomplish. #44Forever

Dedication

This book is dedicated to those amazing people in the world who motivate young people to be exceptional, challenge their conditions, and cultivate their individual voices.

Special thanks to all those people not afraid to be true to themselves in the face of isolation or oppression; the world would not be the same without you. You will be rewarded for your loyalty and dedication to self.

Final salute in advance for those who will purchase this book and share with someone who can activate its advice. It takes rebels like you to make a difference in another soul's life for the better.

Dear Elijah,

By the time that you can read this letter you would have heard most of these words. It is important nonetheless to share these thoughts with you as I reflect on our first eight years together. It is safe to say that we grew up together, because I was very much so a child when I had you. There has been so many lows and highs over the years, but I would not change a thing. I wish there was a way to capture the enormity of the emotion that I have felt in our time together but I do not have the words. Funny thing about life, when you are going through it you do not feel much of anything except immense passion. It is the same passion that I hope you possess along your way and it is my prayer that I serve as motivation for you. It is my ambition that I open every door possible for you so that your every passion can become more than a dream. See this road I trod was stony, and there were plenty of sacrifices, missteps, and failings I had to endure to get us here. So please understand that there is a reason I demand greatness from you. There is an air of expectancy over your life and it will not and cannot be escaped.

When I first had the idea to write this book it did not have the same title nor the same theme. When I first was given the vision, I felt compelled to provide you a guide for living if something were ever to happen to me. Though the concept of the book has changed, the goal has not. What you are reading is the fourth composition of this same text and each previous version was thrown out. Why did I pitch those versions? Because I did not trust that it was good enough for you. I was not positive that those words would guide your daily walk and order your steps, if by chance God saw fit to have me join him.

I had to be sure as well that I was the man I needed to be to write them; not just for you, but for the world. I know that every young son looks up to his father as the epitome of manhood, as I did with your K-Pa, but I had some growing up to do. I had some demons to exorcise and trials to overcome in order to be that person for you.

I wrote this book as part guide and part autobiography so that you could understand who your father was and the process to develop into who you know now. As a 27-year-old man nearing a decade of fatherhood, I felt I was ready to give the world and you this text. Not because I can confidently say that I have it all figured out or that I am some sort of guru, but simply because I am a seasoned father and dedicated servant to my role as educator.

There is something fundamentally different about the way we, those of us who share our hue and gender, have to navigate this world. By the time you can read this letter, I am positive you have more than my warnings as evidence of this fact. None of us are immune from the negative perceptions or biases that we have been burdened with. You can never be responsible for them or take ownership for how they make you feel; that is the world we live in. Remember that God never gives you more than you can handle, and this too applies to your journey as a Black man in America.

I pray that by now you are an avid history lover and that you have found innumerable examples of what a Black man can do in this world. If nothing else, I hope you forever maintain your memories of Granddaddy, who was 103 or 104 when you were running around at his feet. I never for a moment thought he would live to know and love my son; that should be example enough. By now you realize that we, Collins men, have had a very unique experience, because it has been mainly men in our clan.

If it were not for your great-grandfather's example and your great-grandmother's prayers, our family, I, and you by default, would be in a very different place in this world. It is my hope that you can see this as a lesson of what is and will always be the most important thing in life: your family.

Not saying that we will ever be perfect, or that we will not or have not caused you any frustration and pain, but we are always here and we will always love you. It is important that I teach you that. It is important that you teach your son that. It is important to know that you can cry and you can fail and you can disappoint, yet you are still loved. It is important that I tell and teach you this because I can never expect the world to do so. It is not in its nature to love you in the way you need to be loved. There is this perception that we are in some way subhuman and need less than others. Though we have survived centuries with less, it does not mean that we deserve or require less.

Love is the foundation; it is where it all begins for us. It is what we crave and what we seek at all costs though it is so very hard to find in the world. That is why you have to start from inside yourself to seek it, which is why it is my job to plant that seed there. That seed will become something much more than you or I can ever imagine. That seed is what God uses to help you find your passion.

Kahlil Gibran wrote," Love is work made visible," and from that work flows God. So when you embark upon this journey called life you have to know what drives you. You should know what brings you joy and what causes you anger.

There is nothing more important than for you, Black boy, to know who you are in this world. Your words can never define you because you will solely be judged by your actions. You cannot expect the benefit of the doubt. You cannot feel entitled to anything in this world because for you, and everyone else born without privilege, you must earn it.

So, you must know where you are headed and what you want to achieve and how you are going to find success by any means necessary. Son, it is important that you know who you are so that no one else can ever try to define you. It is your behavior that will make a difference on who you can become. No one can ever be more responsible for who you become than you yourself. So, you should work hard to become a great man. You must work nonstop to achieve the success or anything else that you desire.

Moreover, I want you to know that I believe that you have been a blessing in my life since the moment you entered it. There were times when I was afraid about what was in store for us, but it made us stronger. It may seem at times that I am not understanding you or not willing to listen, but this could not be further from the truth.

Funny thing is that you are so much like me that it is scary.

For that reason, I know EXACTLY what you are thinking and most, if not all, of the wild thoughts and ideas that pop into your head. I just call it karma or God paying me back, but I expect you to give me quite a bit a grief; I gave it to my dad. Yet, there was always an understanding that I was always going to do what was right at the end of the day. It did not always happen and I was far from perfect, but he grew to trust that I was focused on where I had to go and my responsibility to be successful.

No matter what happens in our future, I want you to know that I am always going to be with you, if not physically, through the lessons that I have taught you. I know that without a doubt that you are destined for great things, and you have the capacity to accomplish whatever you wish if you commit yourself to it.

I know that there will be dark days but I also know that the sun will shine more often in your life. It may seem at times that I come down on you unjustly, but I know what kind of world that we live in, and what it takes to make it to this point in life. I will tell you explicitly it is not possible if you never learn to control your emotions, to challenge your biases, and to develop thick skin.

We are Black males in America and we must be willing to shoulder that burden. Luckily for us, we come from greatness, we are descendants of the original man, we have royalty flowing through our veins. We can harness that power and use it to our benefit if we so choose, but you do not have an option.

I think back to the time I told K-Pa that your mom was pregnant and the shocked, disappointed look on his face. As you know, we had the same journey of having a child while in college, and later Micah and Mason were conceived when your Uncle Cam was in his senior year. For the record, you CANNOT have a child in college, time to break up this generational trend... seriously. Albeit, I knew that it would be a long journey and it would change everything about my life.

I remember the next day we lost our angel, your great-grandfather, and I knew then that there was nothing I could to better honor his legacy then raising you properly. No, our situation was not and is not yet perfect, but I do know that I am committed to providing the example you need to become a great man. I do not believe that I would be a good steward of my responsibility as a father, if I do not demonstrate success.

The success that I garner is what will make you hungry for something similar. I know that you can never be anything more than the examples that you are exposed to. It is my moral duty to raise you in a manner that will be conducive to future success. If there is one thing that K-Pa did was make sure that we were well-rounded young men; renaissance men.

I truly want to thank you for making me a better man. I knew that I had to put a lot of childish things away, and I tell you all the time that we grew up together. We found a way to get to this point and if there was no path in sight, we made one. I have so much faith in what God is going to do in your life, because He did it for me as well. I know that you have a little bit of Reverend Collins in you from your few months together in heaven. I know that you have been endowed with just a touch of his foresight and I see it manifested daily.

I truly believe that you are a special little boy and I know that all your family and loved ones see it as well. I just pray that I will be around to see you become a father and well-established in your career; it would be my life's joy. I have said this on several occasions that I know I will have more kids, but there will always be something special about our connection. That I will always have a personal affection for you unlike anything with anyone. No matter what happens from this point forward, I want you to know that you will always be my little man and I will always be your big man.

Love Always,
Daddy

"I'm for truth, no matter who tells it. I'm for justice,
no matter who it's for or against."
-Malcolm X

"A man is a success if he gets up in the morning and goes to
bed at night and in between does what he wants to do."
-Bob Dylan

"I'm stomping in my own lane. I'm doing what I do."
-Nasir Jones

"Nothing stops a man who desires to achieve. Every obstacle is
simply a course to develop his achievement muscle."
-Thomas Carlyle

"I want to be the voice of the people; black, white, everyday
oppressed people. A person trying to make it and to do it right."
-Common

"If you do not conquer self, you will be conquered by self."
-Napoleon Hill

"I'm a real rebel with a cause."
-Nina Simone

Rebel Beginnings

"Whenever you find yourself on the side of the majority, it is time to pause and reflect."

-Mark Twain

If you do not have opponents to the way that you think then you will struggle to significantly impact the world around you. There is a serious misconception in our society today that informs people that they should go along to get along, or that change is something that should not be fought for. There seems to be this widespread assumption that the vehicle of revolution is fueled by peaceful coexistence. Frederick Douglass, devoted abolitionist and intellectual giant, acknowledged, "Power concedes nothing without a demand. It never did and it never will." These words are a testament of an age-old understanding that nothing or no person in control of any situation will ever surrender without being forced to do so. The premise of this book contends that independent revolution is necessary for any man to be able to break the chains that obstruct his or her life.

There has been a fundamental shift in what it means to be a rebel, and the meaning of rebellion itself. The images of Fonzie from Happy Days, Will Smith from Fresh Prince, or other fictional characters that stood firm against stereotypical authority figures were the gold standard for what a rebel was all about. In society, this once looked like the kids who said, "NO" to homework, study groups, or the Honor Roll/Dean's List who smoked cigarettes, had sex early, did not graduate high school, and often those who were overall defiant toward authority. This is no longer the case because we have entered a new era of what makes you a viable asset in a society firmly planted in the knowledge economy. The funny thing about this economy is that it requires knowledge. Ignorance only prepares you for a life of unfulfilling work and undervalued service. This is not how you want to live out the adult years of your life, all because you listened to the lies that your environment told you.

It is for these reasons that I was compelled to write this guide. It is for the generations of people who have been misled, miseducated, and manipulated into believing that what they had to offer was not worthy of consideration. Those who have suffered the indignity of having someone convince them that they had no vision and no chance to succeed. This book is specifically for you.

For everyone who has struggled to rage against self-doubts and fears of inadequacy; this book speaks to your situation. Those people who have had amazing ideas, yet faced repeated failure; this will change your fortune or, at least, your perspective. I was forced to change mine or it would have always been a hindrance to my success. This shift in attitude was to enhance my own understanding of my past to ensure that it did not incarcerate my present and shatter the dreams of my future.

This manuscript is also for those of us who have achieved success on one level or another yet are beginning to become complacent. It is for those who have benefited greatly from their efforts in the past but live as if that time has not passed on. I speak to the hearts of all those who are wondering how they can reach their next level or become truer versions of themselves. It is for all those people who believe the idea that you, "get good grades, get in a good school, get a good job, and get to retirement" no longer speaks to the Millennial generation. I write this for everyone who has tried to reinvent themselves only to be held back by the possibility of failure. The words to follow are for everyone who has been told they are too old to change or too young to comprehend. I simply want to speak to the spirits of people who know, deep in their hearts, that there must be a better way.

REBEL was written as an instruction manual to change the way we have been systematically taught to think. It is an attempt to unlock the dormant potential in every person, young and old, to better interpret the conditions that contribute to the reality they face. This is not another book to read and place on your shelf. This is to be read, reflected upon, read again, and then mastered until you assemble the pieces of your life together as you see fit. This is an invitation to become a true thinker, and eventually a visionary who is incapable of small thinking. It is my mission to open minds about the possibility of living sustainably and thinking independently. This book is not about writing what others will agree with, it is about teaching others to find their own truth. The preeminent creative mind of the 21st century, thus far, was Steve Jobs, and he had these words to share:

> *"Your time is limited, so don't waste it living*
> *someone else's life. Don't be trapped by dogma*
> *– which is living with the results of other*
> *people's thinking. Don't let the noise of others'*
> *opinions drown out your own inner voice."*

If you never learn to trust your inner voice than you will only go as far as someone else allows, which is imprisoned by their imagination and is safe for their ego. We have the responsibility to ourselves to live boldly and unapologetically realizing our full potential. By any means necessary.

A popular quote is that "if you don't take time to build your dreams someone will hire you to build theirs." Once we climb the mental mountain and elevate our consciousness about our position in a company, we understand that someone once dreamt all that you see and willed it to life. They were not smarter, stronger or better than you in anyway, but they were likely more developed, hungrier, and driven enough to execute their vision. They were not comfortable waiting for what they wanted but rather honest with themselves about what they could tolerate in their life; dreamlessness was not one of those things.

President Barack Obama on the campaign trail uttered these words, "Change will not come if we wait for some other person or some other time. We are the ones we've been waiting for. We are the change that we seek." The reality about change is that it is inevitable, but real, sustainable change will almost always require the dedication to see it through regardless of the circumstances.

So, as you read, keep in mind that you have somewhere to be, something to do, and someone who is depending on you accomplishing your goals. Overstand being a rebel will not be easy, it will not be pleasant at times, it will likely cause you to be isolated, but it will be worth it. It will bring peace and it will be transformational. Whether you succeed or not will not hurt you as much as the regret that will come from missed opportunities that would have changed your life. J. Cole uttered on a track that "...only thing worse than death is a regret-filled coffin. So, try before you die or always wonder what if..."; it is crunch time, rebel.

Most transformational opportunities are lost by not wanting to leave our comfort zone, by not refusing the easy road. The moment of truth for me was when I realized that what was between my ears was the only hindrance to the fulfillment of my purpose. I do my best now to live with a rebel state of mind. One that stands up to every fear and requires that I move aggressively in the pursuit of my dreams. In a remix of the famed saying by international icon and boxing legend Muhammad Ali, I say "Rebel, young man, rebel!"

In My Lifetime

This book should have been written four years ago or so I thought. It was supposed to have been changing the lives of hundreds or thousands or millions of people by now; that is what I imagined for it. The truth is that I was not the man I needed to be to write such an impactful book. I still had to endure the refining process that life takes you through before I could be the most effective servant to others. It took me learning that everything in life requires a process. There are no secret formulas or magic potions that will allow for you to become the best person you can be. Take it from me you do not want to have to learn that the hard way, even though chances are you will. There is nothing new under the sun. Know that.

It is something about wisdom and youth that always clash

and contend with each other. Part of the problem is that in your youth, you believe that you are invincible, and that you have all the time in the world to make mistakes and recover from them. There is a sense of fearlessness and an uncontrolled drive that forces you to move without consideration of all the consequences, whether good or bad, positive or negative.

Simply put, you do not know what you do not know. Wisdom, on the other hand, requires that you become more of a cerebral or thinking person before you act. It demands that you develop control over your thoughts and mandates that you mentally process *before* you physically move. In your youth, the wisdom that is shared from parents and elders sounds like they are being overly cautious and unnecessarily prudent. We may not like their approach, but this is just their way of telling you that there is a process that must be considered before you act. Nothing more or less.

Whenever you are faced with the challenges life throws your way you must be willing to take the *necessary* steps. There is always something more for you. More of what you may ask? Well, more of anything and more of everything that this world has to offer you! Whether you want to be more skilled in a sport or profession or want to be a better husband or father or student or one-handed juggler, we all must endure the process that is required to make that happen. The distance between your wildest dreams and your present reality is only the process of growth that you must pass through. This process is a tedious one and will require that you develop yourself in many ways which we will get into a little later.

Just know that the basis for growth and transformation always starts with what is between your ears. To change one's mind is the simplest and most difficult thing anyone must decide to do.

Everything in my life changed when I began celebrating that I was not like everyone else. I am different from you. You are different from me. We are all uniquely individual, born with the capacity to become whatever we would like if we are willing to fight for it. Once you can fully appreciate your individuality, then and only then, can you truly find peace and purpose in your life. Too often people attempt to become like everyone around them and it works against them. I love the idea that I am different from everyone else around me, and you should love that fact about yourself as well. Not because it makes me better in any way, but because it is a declaration that I do me better than anyone else. Teddy Roosevelt wrote that, "comparison is the thief of joy," and frankly he was right. We live in an age of mass produced goods, widespread social norms, and prejudice-laden stereotypes. All of this is made possible because we have compared one another to such a great extent that we find it hard to be openly accepting of our differences. It is through these differences that we can find the people who are true complements to our life i.e. where I am weak, you are strong, and vice versa. This is particularly keen when deciding upon a spouse, and progression in career because who can love you or your work if you do not first love you and it yourself?

To be able to answer this question, I overcame years of wandering around silent and blind mucking through the triumphs, failures, and pain of my past. In this section, I want to share my testimony with you, the reader, so that you further grasp that your circumstance does not determine your capacity for growth. Everyone has a story, each soul has their own anguish, and every person's conscience has been torn between present circumstances and past unresolved issues. No one is exempt from this and it is perfectly natural. Much like everyone has the same 24 hours in a day, we each have our own personal struggles that must be overcome before we can truly begin loving ourselves fully. There are a few pivotal steps that must be taken to position yourself to become the truest version of you.

First, it would be unwise to pretend that pain and struggle are not a normal process to your life because they are and you must get over it. You cannot get discouraged about trials, but rather become solution-oriented and make the necessary steps to correct the current issue. This will always begin with acknowledging that you *cannot* control what has already happened in your life, and deciding that you are not a victim. What happened to you destroyed other people but it could not beat you. In the words of heralded theologian and Morehouse Man, Howard Thurman: "What happens to you cannot defeat you unless you allow it to get in you." My suggestion? Hang this quote on your wall until you believe it. It changed my perspective on life.

Next, you should put protections in place to guard against repeating the same mistakes. Nothing can continuously happen to you without your acceptance on some level. Therefore, you must be willing to see every mistake as a learning opportunity. A chance for you to adjust, and try again with your new strategy. If you are not going to be proactive about changing what caused your mistake, then you can never be mad about it; at some point, you must own it. Anyone who owns a business will tell you that they were responsible for whatever happened, even if it was not something they directly did. Why? Because they understand that if you make excuses you will live your life as a victim and victims are rarely accountable for their behavior. Victims never succeed for long because they are intoxicated with the idea of being someone's step stool.

The last step, once you are on the other side of any trial, is to objectively reflect on how the situation could have come out differently. This is the simplest thing to do, but often the hardest one to complete. Most people would rather block out what happened instead of thinking about it intensely. Remember that anyone who has a problem reflecting on their past is destined to repeat those same mistakes in their future.

This is why I wanted to share these few steps to help you better process this singular universal truth: *It is the culmination of our experiences and how we interpret them that determines how our past can become fuel or fetters for our future greatness.* To provide further perspective for these rules I want to dissect my life to show you how you can apply them to your situation.

The first rule again is that you cannot pretend that the pain is not real. Ironically, this is the exact thing that I did for years about several things that happened in my childhood that I did not come to grips with until I was 17 years old or later. Before I start, I want to let it be known that I loved growing up, and the people I was surrounded with. I cannot say that we, my older brother and I, had everything, but we wanted for nothing. Our middle-class upbringing was seemingly perfect, and we were placed in countless life-enriching activities that propelled us to greater heights. I would be lying to say that I hated the cards I was dealt, but the reality is that I hid so much pain from my elders and friends that I felt I was walking alone in the world. I am sure many of you feel the same way, and that there is nothing that can be done about it. For the record, I disagree with you and the little voice in the back of your head telling you that "there is nothing that can be done to fix it."

I should note that for the first seven years of my life, I lived in absolute bliss. There was never an instance where I wanted anything, can remember any significant pain (outside of chicken pox and those oatmeal baths), or was faced with any sort of serious adversity. My mother was absolutely amazing, and she deserves immense credit for my mental development as a small child, which we know now is the most pivotal time for a child's learning. We had family vacations, participated in everything from Boys Scouts to library book clubs, and had the privilege of living in a home with both parents. This segment of my life I have no interest in discussing, because frankly did little to develop my character or aid my transition into a rebel later in life. This is when I lived the cookie cutter life, and did not understand the notion of struggle, strife, or strain. I was part of the stereotypical image for the "stable Black family." However, the waves of change were about to blow my little castle in the sand away.

Society, too often, confuses financial stability or other superficial aspects of life as the measuring stick to whether someone's life is difficult. It is pure foolishness to think that way because of how misleading it is. The man who taught me the game of basketball, Donald Powell Sr., said, "I know garbage men who live better lives than bankers. Your job or money does not mean you are happier than anyone else." It took years to understand what he meant but it was a lesson that stayed with me for all these years.

Thus, never judge anyone by his/her cover or from a superficial lens, because it will only hinder your vision, and leads away from true understanding. This is the foundation of bias and should always be kept in check, but that too will be discussed later. With this, we start to unwrap the perils of my early childhood and the fact that I could have easily not been here to share this story with you.

The Other Carlton

Growing up in the 90s was a special experience for me, because I was always compared to a well-known and highly-public TV character Carlton Banks from the Fresh Prince of Bel-Air. This young man was the son of a deeply intellectual, pro-Black college professor and activist turned lawyer then judge, who lived in a mansion in California with a penchant for the finer things in life. He had a style all his own and lived unapologetically, though he questioned it at times, in his own lane, yet was consistently ostracized simply for being his corny self. It did not help that I was not yet two years old when the program launched in 1990, but even

23 years later I still get the same response whenever I say my name.

In hindsight, I am grateful for the comparison and having to live in his shadow, though fictional, because I, ironically, embody some of the same experiences. He was often the smartest Black kid, if not the only black kid, in his honors classes, was teased for his intellect, reared by a strong father who preached the value of education, he sung all the time, and he developed a code of conduct that very much beat to his own drum. But the similarities end there. There was no silver spoon, no mother (in my pre-adolescent and adolescent years), and definitely no dancing! If I had a dollar for every time someone asked me to do that silly dance, I would dethrone Bill Gates for wealthiest man in the world. Easy. Long story short, we shared very little outside of the name, thus I was always, *The Other Carlton*.

We are going to dive head first into the darkest period of my life, which was from ages 8-17. These are the years that a child is supposed to live with limited worries, and fully embrace his/her right to develop carefree; keyword: supposed. In my case, it all began with the divorce of my parents when I was seven, and how everything transpired after that point. It was much like a 7.0 earthquake pointed directly at my heart, where the foundation was shaken then split wide open.

Like most parents in that situation, my father sat us down when we were visiting him in Chicago and said that, "Your mom and I are getting a divorce." We gave the customary response of crying but, for some odd reason, when he told me that it was not our fault, I believed him instantly, and saw it as problems between adults. (For the record, I do not want to rehash every detail about the past, but I do want to paint a full picture for you even though some did not shape my current consciousness.)

Fast forward to after my father moved out, that was when we were placed on a visitation schedule with weekdays spent with our mom and weekends with our father. This was mostly the standard because my mother worked every weekend anyway as a registered nurse, my father as a project manager for a national construction firm. Everything was calm, relatively speaking, until my mother got a new boyfriend, who convinced her that we were "unruly boys."

From that moment on, everything in our lives changed. Our mother, to that point, had never physically disciplined us, but after her newfound mate made an utterance of disapproval that all changed. Unfortunately, there was not equity in the dispersal of the abuse, for my brother it started much earlier. I was able to dodge the abuse for a few months, but that did not last long at all. Though I did have a knack for not repeating the same mistakes of those who came before me.

It is still hard to fathom how a mother can rationalize beating her children at the bequest of another man, but that is something I am done trying to figure out. Keep in mind while you reflect on your past that you will *only* waste valuable time and energy trying to understand the thought processes of another person. It is more important to grasp how that behavior made you feel and shaped your consciousness. Long story short, we were beat for everything imaginable, i.e. missing trash can liners, a dirty dish, not finishing food, forgetting to turn off light switches, etc. This was outside of the customary behaviors that most kids got in trouble for like talking back or trouble in school, which I deem appropriate. It took years to consider all the methods of abuse that we were faced with but I slowly began to see the full picture.

The psychological abuse was probably the worst to deal with because our punishments were cumulative. So, after the infraction occurred we would receive a writing assignment for it, usually somewhere between 200-500 sentences that were always given a time limit that, if failed, carried a beating. That, for most parents, would have been enough, but each violation carried a certain number of hits that were to be dealt on Friday; right before we were to be sent to our father.

It was always the longest walk home off the bus knowing that I had a beating waiting on me, because I forgot to replace a liner or some other small mistake. I remember having to count out our hits as they happened and if we missed a number it would be repeated. There were plenty other "rules" to our punishments, but to be honest, I do not want to think about how the abuse happened anymore. Why? Because no matter how much I tell you it will not benefit your understanding of how to overcome pain. Plus, why add insult to injury to the name of my mother? She is already forgiven and knowing the truth of what she did to her children is punishment enough, or it should be. I do consider how reading this or having it shared with her will make her feel. It is my fervent prayer that she has already forgiven herself and can read these words as facts leading to a deeper truth. Nonetheless, we move on.

The key moment during this time was when we, my mother,

her boyfriend, my brother, and I, sat at the dinner table discussing some frivolous topic, as we often did. Then there was some discrepancy over what I said and what the boyfriend heard me say. Over and over he made the claim that I was lying with me passionately disagreeing.

My mother at once silenced me and told me that I was lying "because an adult had said so." That night was the worst beating I ever received, but more importantly, I never looked at my mother the same again. No matter what, I always believed that she would never put anyone before her baby boy. To a degree, I had internalized the abuse and accepted my responsibility for my punishments, yet when I did nothing wrong I could no longer believe I had ever done anything wrong. From then on, I could not own what was happening, and I could not carry its responsibility. Essentially, I became a victim and operated with that mentality.

Repeatedly, we would face our scheduled abuse until one day we came to my grandmother's house in tears, which prompted a sit down with my father. Hesitantly, we told him everything that had been happening and it spawned a call to 241-KIDS and a visit from Child Protective Services.

It was one of the most terrifying experiences of my childhood because unlike now when there is reported abuse the child is separated from the accused by law; back in '97 this was not the case. Thus, we sat answering questions from the social worker while staring at the angry gaze of our mother, so we lied.

We lied about what was happening out of fear from the woman who gave us life; it is still sobering to think that that was my reality during those years. The feeling of fear dissipated when we got back to our father's house that weekend, and we could visibly see his concern and shame that he could not protect his most prized possessions, his children. This would soon no longer be a concern.

It was sometime in September, I remember it was not long after school year began, and my brother got in trouble in his 5th grade class. The expectation as we walked from the bus stop was that he would be beaten per custom, but when we reached the house, my mother's approach was shockingly different.

A discussion ensued that concluded with her demanding that my brother leave and to go live with my father. She quickly packed him a bag and sent him to my grandmother's (who lived at the bottom of the hill). The entire time I sat silent in our room, emotionless, and in shock by the turn of events until my brother walked out the door.

At that moment, I realized that I was all alone without anyone I trusted to rely on. During the entire situation, no matter what, my brother was at my side, next to me facing the same trials, we encouraged each other; he was my haven in the house, and I was his. Fear consumed me at that moment.

Roughly about an hour after my brother had his bag packed and was sent away, my mother came to me and asked the question, "Are you going to leave me too?" With terror, confusion, and loneliness welling up through the tears that fell from my eight-year-old eyes I responded, "I don't want to be without my brother." So, she subsequently packed a bag for me and sent me out the door as well.

After that we were legally required to spend Monday, Wednesday, and Friday evenings with our mother from 4-9PM. Things changed for a period, and it seemed like she was to be trusted once more. This change was very short lived as many of the same things continued to happen.

The only person I was ever fully honest with was my Uncle Mitchell, my father's brother, who was the younger of two boys like I was. He became my trusted advisor, but he also coached me through everything, including pep talks, before and after, I was beaten on several occasions. Once the abuse continued we began to dodge our scheduled visits with our mother by staying outside and remaining out of sight for the entire 4-9pm visit. There was a claim that made it back to family court that my father was intentionally keeping us away from her, therefore we went back to the schedule to keep our father out of trouble. One day in the not too distant future from that point, we stopped going altogether and stopped hiding our dissatisfaction with going to visit her. After that point, we were no longer forced as we no longer cared to receive the same treatment.

For months, we had gone without seeing our mother outside of the occasional drive-by as we played outside on Morning Glory. I remember making a game out of hiding from her as we saw her approach, not understanding that this was hurtful towards her. But I was legitimately nervous anytime I was around her. This continued throughout the summer of '98, and eventually we stopped going toward the top of our street altogether.

One fall day, I remember my father sitting us down and sharing news with us about our mother's departure. He told us that she had moved nearly 2,000 miles across the country to Tucson, Arizona with her boyfriend. That anything we had left in the house was gone and that he was unsure when we would see her again. At that very moment, the only question that repeated in my mind was "Why didn't she say goodbye?"

For years I pondered this question, I shed countless tears while coping with the harsh reality that the woman who gave life to me never cared enough about her children to even embrace them before she left. Because I received so much positive reinforcement from my father and other family members, it never impacted my self-esteem or caused deeper issues like most people who deal with that kind of trauma, but it did not stop the pain.

For months on end, I cried about my mother not loving me, questioning why she changed from the woman I knew for the first seven years of my life. Just as I began to cope with her absence the first loss of a loved one, furthermore changed the course of my life. Nothing has ever been the same since.

Reasonable Doubt

I woke up early in the morning headed into my fourth-grade class ready to pass out my Valentine's Day cards to classmates, collect mine in return, and eat plenty of candy. It was always one of my favorite holidays to celebrate in school because everyone always seemed so excited to be enjoying the day especially my teachers who had all been female to that point.

We went to our grandmother's house after school as we always did, and had a relatively calm evening before my dad arrived to pick us up. As we were headed home, my father received a call from my grandfather on his cell that prompted us to head back. My father was unsure what was wrong, thus as we came in he directed us toward the basement and instructed us to turn the TV on and wait for his call. As we walked through the living room, I heard my grandmother crying loudly, and grandfather comforting her so I knew something was terribly wrong.

After about half an hour, we were called to the top of the steps by our father, and directed to sit down and face him. It was a very surreal moment because I am sure that there were plenty of consoling words that my father shared with us in that moment, but I only remember 13 of them. First, he told us that "your Uncle Mitchell passed away," which shot an intense pain through my entire body and all I could do was cry profusely. After a short while he sent us back downstairs with the eight words that shaped my adolescence, "Be strong. Do not let Grandma see you cry." I do not know why those words affected me so deeply, but I carried them with me throughout that week and the rest of my childhood.

At the time, my grandfather was pastor of one of the most influential churches in Cincinnati, thus we had tons of people bringing food, sending condolences, and offering aid at the house. Every day we came from school with a new group of people in the house to hug us and tell us how sorry they were for our loss; none of it mattered.

I wore my fictitious smile and did all I could to be of

assistance, but I had never felt so alone in my life. I felt alone because my uncle, my father's brother, was my refuge, my guide, and he gave me so much encouragement in those years. I never felt more incomplete to that point in my life, thus I cried everywhere out of view of my grandmother, including at school and particularly in bed each night. It was not until about Thursday night that I began to feel any better, because family started to arrive into town.

That is when I gained the understanding that death is not always a bad thing, because it brings families closer together. I was not at peace, though, until my sister walked through the door and I felt her embrace, because she was the dearest person in the world that I had left.

The rest of the weekend was a family-filled blur, but I vividly remember all the faces in attendance, and tears I shed on the day of the funeral. Civil rights legend, Rev. Fred L. Shuttlesworth was the eulogist. He was also the one who baptized my uncle and father while he was pastor of the church, Revelation Missionary Baptist, my grandfather was currently at the helm of. There were plenty of key figures in the city there to pay their respects, but all I could think of was that I had no one to share my fears with. Everything was okay for that weekend, but once everyone departed I understood that I was truly lost. Seemingly, I had no one to turn to and there was no aid in sight.

After the close of that weekend all that remained were the words of my father and the hollow feeling that I had no one I could confide in. It was in that time that I seemingly lost all the encouragement that helped me make it through the trials with my mother. There was a tsunami of emotion that flooded my soul every night for nearly two months until one night I told myself that "you cannot cry anymore." So, I made a couple decisions that altered my mindset and dictated my behavior for the next half dozen or so years.

First, I determined that my love for my mother was the reason that I was still crying, thus I made a conscious effort to hate her instead. Secondly, since I lost my confidant, I figured that I was meant to deal with my issues alone. These two beliefs lead me to presume that I could not afford to love or trust anyone, nor was I supposed to be vulnerable any longer. It also gave me a considerable distrust for women, because my coping method was rooted in hatred versus forgiveness or understanding. This was by far the most shadowy phase of my life where the light, the same one that everyone has, was greatly dimmed.

This was the time of my life where I felt that no one understood me and that no matter what I did, no matter what accolades I collected, I could never fill the void of what was lost. Then the changes I made in my psyche began to show up in my everyday life in the form of anger. This anger manifested itself in many different forms towards everyone and everything. There was hatred for my brother because we argued as kids always do, hatred toward my father for being a stern disciplinarian, directed at my grandparents due to their insistence on morality and decorum, all over school as the token Black child in all-white honors classes, and the list goes on. I was 10 with only one intimate experience with death in my entire life, but I felt that it would have been easier to simply join my uncle in heaven.

One night after being punished for some infraction in school (and there were many), I lied awake staring at the ceiling searching for a reason to live. I sat wondering if anyone would miss me if I simply killed myself and was never to be seen or heard from again. I visualized all the faces close to me. And all I saw was their disapproval and viewed them through my misplaced hatred toward them. Confusion was my master, and I thought I had little control.

The scariest part, in reflection, was that I knew how to load the shotgun that my father had and where he stored it. Therefore, I knew how I would make my exit. At the last moment, right when I reached the guns hiding place, the image of my sister crying shot into mind and I was halted in my tracks. The only thought that passed through my head repeatedly is that, "I cannot hurt her like this." So, I retreated to bed and cried until my eyes were too heavy to keep open with anger that I could not let go.

There is one lesson that is worthwhile in sharing, which I hope will be able to help others, is that death is the foundation and catalyst of new life. It is not meant for us to understand fully, but rather we have the obligation to come to terms with its existence.

Childish Gambino, one of the hottest artists/actors/creatives, said in one of his songs, "that it's funny that the day you're born you're given a death sentence." Truer words were never spoken, because we all will pass away one day; we all must cope with that reality. Furthermore, we have an individual responsibility to live our lives in a way where we can realize our dreams, work our passion and live on purpose.

The saddest thing, if I had pulled the trigger, would not have been that I died, but that I never gave myself a chance to live. My life would have ended abruptly but I would have altered the lives of so many people that I have grown to love, support, and guided over the years. Thus, no matter how bad the situation you must keep the mindset that you are only a victim if you allow yourself to be. No one has that control over your life.

When considering the high number of suicides there are in America, there are two principal issues that should frame your understanding. Initially, there was a false belief that my circumstance was greater than my capacity to fix it; there is a lack of faith in my own and God's strength. After that, a deeper and more telling truth is that they did not love themselves.

This at once begs the question of "who can love you or your work if you do not first love yourself?" I do not want to go too deep into this as we will discuss it further in later chapters, but you should not be afraid of death, but fear not ever truly being alive. The iconic Benjamin Franklin spoke about this saying, "Some people die at 25 and aren't buried until 75." As a person, grateful to have made it to see his 27th birthday, I have made a conscious decision to live fully, and I write this guide to help others do the same. Regardless of what the world tells you that you are capable of, make liars out of them.

There are plenty more stories I could share in this period that were filled with anger and destructive behaviors that occurred, but what good would it do? I feel it is more pertinent to share that my intellect, socioeconomic status, or rich religious background offered no shelter from struggle.

Pain and resentment and fear and doubt and loneliness are all feelings that everyone must deal with at some point of their lives. You cannot buy a different result, there is no amount of begging or pleading that can be done to avoid its visit, your only recourse is to be well-equipped to face these issues head on. Every person should be developing a toolkit, a set of thoughts, behaviors, and a belief system that they can draw inspiration from to keep the flame of hope burning bright inside.

Famous author and biographer Alex Haley wrote, "In every conceivable manner, the family is link to our past, bridge to our future." Without a proper understanding of how your childhood shaped, and still informs, your thinking then you will never be able to fully comprehend your current situation or what your future holds.

I wanted to be intentional as you read and we journey together through this book, that you fully understand that you do not have to be ashamed of what you have overcome, or are still dealing with. I wanted to make it clear that there is no reason to ever regret anything in your life if you learn from the experience.

I did not feel that this book could be impactful unless I shared myself with you as I wrote it, and you have something to identify with as you read. I subscribe to the words of the late-poetess and titanic figure, Maya Angelou, when she told us to, "Try to be a rainbow in someone else's cloud." I share because I realized early in life that I was built to conquer whatever life threw my way. I had the tolerance, the fortitude, the strength and the innate ability to survive anything, and you have it too. Not that I was special or endowed with unique skill, but because I had hope for a brighter future, faith in better tomorrows, and by constantly seeking to give (in my later years) and receive love. It made all the difference and it will for you as well.

From ages 9-17 was the foundation of how my life as a rebel began; it is my cornerstone. Any building is only as strong as the foundation beneath that it stands on. Since you are already here, growing and learning, you must dig deep within yourself and repair all the cracked areas in your foundation. The house, your life, cannot hold the weight of anymore strain without healing first. Though you cannot change what happened, you do have the power to transform your understanding of the past. This greater comprehension is something that will forever alter your mind, benefit your heart, and encourage your spirit. It is a necessary step in your development as a rebel, because it acknowledges where you can draw strength from.

Thus, as we continue I want to give you applicable skills to be able to make a proper transition into becoming a more complete rebel. It is not easy and there will be sacrifices that need to be made, but the good news is that you are never alone on your journey. There is always someone near or far that will support your dreams as long as you are adamant about accomplishing them. Passion is the greatest sales tool anyone can possess. This is what I want to help you unleash as you translate REBEL into your life.

I write to help you find your purpose through the renewing of your mind. Nevertheless, it will require renovation of the inner workings of your thoughts and a proverbial cleansing of how you perceive the world around you. This, for me, took pain, anger, anguish, and much suffering, but that is why I write this for you. So that you do not have to take the route I did. So, to begin our trek through shifting our consciousness we must first destroy what comedian and Renaissance man Steve Harvey calls "stinking thinking." The time is always now for change, so let us commence starting today.

Rebel State of Mind

"The paradox of education is precisely this –that as one begins to become conscious one begins to examine the society in which he is being educated."

-James A. Baldwin

This is a book about turning progressive thought into purposed action for sustainable change. Without this in mind, the book will sound much like a self-help guide with very little purpose in your everyday life. Yet, it is designed to encourage and ignite the fire of deliberate action to change your perception and then your reality.

Therefore, there are several lessons that I want to give you before we dive into the steps to becoming more unapologetically you. I do not promise you that you are going to immediately change your thinking but I want to at least introduce the pathway toward it.

Famed philosopher George Bernard Shaw was quoted proclaiming, "Progress is impossible without change, and those who cannot change their minds cannot change anything." Thus, we all have the responsibility, if we are truly seeking advancement in any area of our lives, to be open to change.

Not only that, but we also have a duty to ourselves to capitalize on every opportunity life provides to better ourselves, even when inconvenient. It is with this hope I am writing this doctrine for enhanced living. For one of the greatest deterrents to progression is the arrogance or the self-loathing to believe that you can no longer learn, change or grow. If you stop doing these things, you are effectively dead.

There are five areas that must be addressed before you will be able to fully understand the words and frameworks in the chapters to follow. If you were to ask anyone on the street to define any of these terms each person would not only have their own definition but would also be willing to critique yours.

Due to their vast and vague nature, I wanted to deliberately capture them for this book, but also to highlight the great depth of each of them. Time and time again I have heard that "common sense isn't common," and reluctantly, with each passing year, I agree more and more with the statement.

Many people have a distorted vantage point of reality that causes their fears to shape their understanding of certain things. I wanted to create or compile objective, operational definitions for the book as key vocabulary. We will lay the groundwork around the following: *Knowledge, Conscience, Time, Education,* and *Purpose.* There will also be several supplementary definitions that we will need to establish how we are going to use these concepts moving forward.

Knowledge

As always, we start with the basics, which are the keys to unlocking your future, the almighty power of knowledge is the first. By definition, as a noun, it is described as "the fact or state of knowing; the perception of fact or truth; clear and certain mental apprehension." Several words of the definition are pivotal to the true understanding of what knowledge is rooted in. First, we have "fact or state," which insinuates that there are two competing variables; one absolute and the other moldable. Furthermore, I think it wise to grasp that whenever you have two options than a choice should be made that encourages progression for your circumstance. If you consistently act on information that shapes your behavior yet it does not yield positive results, you have a bad source. Facts will not work in that case. On the flipside, if the truth is always malleable then you will struggle to have a firm grasp on reality. It all requires a healthy balance.

Secondly, "perception of fact or truth" is a subtler way to say that everyone has control over what he or she determines to be objectively or subjectively accurate. The problem with the history of any person, place or thing is that it is subject to interpretation of the individual telling the tale. No two people perceive the world the same, thus we are all entitled and required, if we aspire towards self-sufficiency, to adopt a policy of personal validation. If we want to become truly independent, we must be comfortable with our inner voice and trust it. Knowledge comes from a lot of places but we must decide how to use it; we own this and always will.

Finally, we have the unclear usage of the words "certain mental apprehension." Its phrasing professes that knowledge, in all its limitlessness, is a deliberate, intentional thing that should be viewed in clarity. This leads me to believe that there is available mental capacity for those who seek understanding through profitable quests for increased knowledge. But that word apprehension caught me off guard, so I decided to unpack the word.

What I found was the description that summarizes the spirit of what it means to be a critical thinker. Apprehension for our purposes is *"acceptance of or receptivity to information without passing judgment on its validity, often without complete comprehension."*

This word, so often overlooked, had the greatest impact on my perception of knowledge. It opened my eyes to the notion that we often collect information without consideration on whether it is healthy or harmful to our psyches. For example, are people really considering what WorldStar Hip-Hop fights are doing to their minds? They do not understand how toxic stress alters the way your brain works and causes you to be in a constant state of panic.

It also requires that we must succumb to the raw reality that we are individually responsible for every perception, influence, prejudice, and/or bias we hold. It mandates a deep-rooted understanding that we are in total control of what occurs in our lives and how we feel about it. All of this is made possible only by determining the attitude that carries you into and out of fresh experiences, oppressive obstacles, and inspiring triumphs. It is our perspective coupled with our attitude that defines our character and is critical to how others perceive us. We must always challenge what others are trying to get us to believe. Simply put, question everything.

Without making a deliberate decision to maintain a positive outlook, also known as hope for better tomorrows or faith, we are hurled into an abyss of negative thoughts which manifest themselves in the physical as depression or destructive or uncontrollable behavior.

This behavior, therefore, becomes the love child of insecurity and self-deprivation, which causes a pattern working against your long-term sustainability in your role i.e. father, student, musician, daughter, preacher, wife, friend, CEO, etcetera, etcetera.

The principle issue with this level of thoughtfulness is that once you familiarize yourself with it, it should make you feel guilty about returning to your old way of thinking. To seek true wisdom any person is required to repeatedly challenge the status quo in their life. It becomes prerequisite, at a certain point, to only see the world through your eyes as a method of protection. Protection against a loss in productivity and detrimental conduct that arises based on some of the negative influences we allow to reside in our spheres of influence.

A common adage used is that "if you're the smartest one in your circle then you need to change your circle," which simply suggests that the people you surround yourself need to challenge you mentally. Consequently, you should always be aware who is in your life and their potential influence, negatively or positively, on your thinking. Obviously, all people are not on the same level, but if they are not adding to your life positively than you have the responsibility to subtract them from your circle or at least limit their influence.

On a famous interview by Jay-Z years back, he mentioned that people said that he changed when he became successful; it was so inspiring it went viral on Instagram. The pearl was a classic and so unbelievably direct which stated, "[They act] Like you worked that hard to stay the same."

The reality is that when you make a conscious decision to think differently or progress your life in a substantial way than you are going to make stagnant people uncomfortable. Marianne Williamson in her famous quote remarked, "There's nothing enlightened about shrinking so that other people won't feel insecure around you." Thus, it is simply easier to dedicate your social time to people who challenge you to grow.

In today's society, we are operating in an economy where knowledge has never been such a precious commodity. Since the advent of the Information Superhighway aka internet, we have been exposed to more viewpoints, more imagery, and there is exponentially more connectivity around the world. Thus, there has never been such an urgency to be able to decipher between what is healthy, viable information and what is senseless or anti-progressive. Therefore, your understanding and value placed on knowledge is critical to your future success and essential to your growth.

Knowledge, as adjective, is defined as "creating, involving, using, or disseminating special information." This is particularly relevant as the world has entered the knowledge economy, where no one person has control on what the world can share, visualize, or support. Every individual has the capacity, even if they choose not to use it, to determine the truth that they accept. The age of group think has been forever and irreparably changed with the advent of social media combined with planned obsolescence in today's economy. So, we are taking the time to discuss how to embrace endless possibilities and negotiate the world deliberately and critically.

If you have picked up this book to embrace that burning desire within yourself that you should be more, do more or stand for more than you have come to the right place. The key question is, "Are you willing to be misunderstood and discounted by those who are content with the world around them?" If you are looking for a cheat sheet to life that will make your existence less offensive than there is little I can do for you. Life is not simple; there is no easy road to success or progress, but there is a secret to attaining it.

First, you must know exactly what it is that you think and what you believe in. Without first being able to articulate original thought, you (and your independence) will always live in the winds that will undoubtedly blow your life in whatever direction it so chooses. Without firmly planted roots, you will always have to deal with inconsistency in your life, which will make it that much harder to grow.

Independent thinking is the critical first step to becoming a person with the ability to define their place in the world. It is essential to develop a voice that is distinctive from the crowd around you. If you cannot hear your inner voice, then it will be impossible to ever determine your own conscious beliefs. You will forever be trapped in a hamster's wheel of opinions of those around you. In this position, you are contracting your life over to the "most influential" to serve their goals in everything you do i.e. family, relationships, work, service, etc. all because you lack the conviction to think for yourself. Foremost, you must accept this as truth (it may not be an absolute, though it was for me) then formulate a plan of action to change it.

This phenomenon is caused for several different reasons that can be easily diagnosed or prescribed to historical facts of one's life. The truth though is that many are just well-conceived excuses that are adopted to accept the consistent outcomes of our lives. The reality is that we have total control over our thoughts and behaviors as well as the progression or digression that comes from them.

It is a matter of fact that we have been endowed with all the ingredients to become positive influencers of the world around us. It is essential to be acutely aware of what past experiences have influenced you and what current interactions still influence your thinking. One can never reach their full capacity unless first they have reconciled their actions with their thoughts. Do not believe for a moment that this process will be simple; not if it is done correctly. To go over one's life with a proverbial red pen evaluating everything from weakness in character to behaviors that lead to failures in life is challenging and takes immense courage; that is why you need a plan.

Conscience

There are two things imperative to change to fulfill your desire to formulate original thought; these are your *conscience* and your *perception of responsibility*. These two ideas are the foundation of your value system and govern the behavior that is directly connected with physical manifestations of progress in your life. For this book, conscience will be defined as the "acquisition of moral beliefs that inform decision-making and guide the operations of one's life."

Furthermore, responsibility is "the obligation to adopt behaviors that serve a desired outcome to further the cause of self or others you serve." These definitions should be considered heavily as you read as well as when reflecting upon your own life. Let us break these down further to ensure that you have clarity on how these either positively or negatively impact your everyday life.

19th century painter Vincent van Gogh stated, "Conscience is a man's compass." In present-day, it could be said that our conscience serves as the GPS for our lives. It is the culmination of our values and morals that determines our *modus operandi* (method of operation) for our lives. If you cannot fully comprehend, openly share, and operate according to a sound conscience than you will remain at a disadvantage in life.

Consider this, can someone else believe in you and/or your ability if you do not have a code of conduct that governs your life? Not a chance. Nonetheless, do not take this personal because there are quite a few contributors to our conscience including the values of our parents, life experiences, and emotional stability while dealing with the cards life has dealt us. But be clear, no matter how hard your road, what you had to deal with, or why you are in the condition that you are in, it remains your responsibility to become a better person. Also remember that it is never too late to start.

Jean Paul writes, "The conscience of children is formed by the influences that surround them; their notions of good and evil are the result of the moral atmosphere they breathe." This summarizes the point that these factors have contributed greatly to the formation of our conscience and guided the adoption of what we perceive as acceptable action. Nonetheless, we should never worry about the condition of our conscience because we, at all times, have the power to change it for better or worse. In fact, it is our responsibility to continuously develop our conscience to further our progress.

Every person on this planet is faced with their own set of circumstances and issues that must be overcome; this is inevitable. Yet, it is our conscience that guides our path through these trying situations. It is our conscience that offers a strategy to putting the issue behind us.

The underlying understanding about being able to change your conscience is that you are acutely conscious of what is going on around you. The truth is that no person without awareness of their surroundings can ever control what happens in them. Moreover, that unaware person has relinquished his/her power over how his/her environment positively or negatively affects them. They are crippling their own capacity to defend their psyche which is a necessity to improve their social, professional, and mental output.

Consciousness, not to be confused with conscience, requires that you have well-developed cognitive skills that will allow for you to process effectively what occurs in your life. This aptitude can only be increased through reflection on how events in your life, past and present, are shaping your mind and thoughts. We will discuss this much more in-depth in the following chapters so we do not have to dive into this concept quite yet. Just know that you must be proactive about it at all times. It will not magically happen.

Education

Has anyone ever told you education only happens in the classroom? That is not likely. Have you been told that because you are not book smart you are somehow inadequate or dumb? If so, please be clear that whoever told you that is ignorant and small-minded. There are no sanctioned and approved methods for the acquisition of knowledge. From its Greek origins, education comes from the word educe, which means "to draw out or bring forth." This should let you know that education is about the transformation from Point A to Point B; it is all about growth and what you can pull out of yourself. One of the greatest minds of our time, Albert Einstein, had this to say, "Education is what remains after one has forgotten what one has learned in school." I am sure that Einstein understood that education is what has been retained after all the facts that did not apply to one's life have been long forgotten.

Therefore, it is terribly important to learn critically; do not simply accept everyone's truth. No other person's truth will be able to walk properly in your shoes; thus, you have the duty to interpret it for yourself. Famed actress and activist Ruby Dee said, "The greatest gift is not being afraid to question," and I am compelled to agree. The knowledge that you have acquired in any field of study or about any viable industry, even those that are illegal, gives you expertise in that area. What sets teachers apart from their students is the amount of knowledge and/or experience that they should share. This is the same for parents, counselors, mentors, friends and elders in our various communities.

"Education is the most powerful weapon which you can use to change the world," the words of the late, great South African President, activist, and most famous political prisoner Nelson Mandela. Thus, you have a power that often goes untapped if you do not use the knowledge you must change the environment that you live in. There are a multitude of things that can be done to begin influencing the minds around you. They can become more positive, more creative, more productive, more spiritual, and more conscious or, on the contrary, they can be more indoctrinated, more passive, more complacent, more ignorant, and learn to accept more failure. When you have knowledge that goes unshared then you are selfishly shackling the consciousness of those around you.

Therefore, NEVER STOP searching for ways to self-educate because as soon as you do you are virtually committing mental suicide. This reveals an important truth: Education is everywhere, and eternal, until you stop seeking it independently. I have to cite another amazing quote from the current King of Hip-Hop, Jay-Z, when he stated, "I'm hungry for knowledge. The whole thing is to learn every day, to get brighter and brighter. That is what this world is about." The beauty in this statement is that it is an admission that no matter what there is always something further to learn and infinite potential to shine if you seek it. There does not have to be limitations on your development and there is no schedule that you are required to adhere to.

American public-school systems operate on an archaic agrarian calendar that was established for the students of yesteryear to get an education and could still help out on the farm. Obviously, our world has changed and with the advent of the supermarket we do not need to operate this way. We can rest assured that it is likely that our education systems will not be changing anytime soon, but we can change how we operate in them. That is only possible if you are hungry for more knowledge and have a desire to shape your conscience.

Secondly, if you still believe there is one way to solve any problem then you must first begin with intentionally deprogramming your mind. This is not your fault, but a consequence of years of indoctrination through media, education, and in some cases religion. We have all fallen victim to the belief that what we ingest is the truth about society; I am here to tell you that it is false at best and often downright offensive. At this point in your life, I would like to cordially invite you to have a cognitive makeover.

Consequently, here is another jewel: If you control what you consume you take control of what you will accept. There must be some accountability for what you watch, listen to, and the views you accept as they will become the sum of what you speak. In too many instances we see students grow up to believe they are stupid, young girls suppose they are worthless, and young boys accept as true they are bad, all because they consistently heard someone tell them such things. Aristotle remarked that, "it is the mark of an educated mind to be able to entertain a thought without accepting it," thus it is time to take it upon yourself to rewrite the truth that you believe about yourself. Remember that education is what you "bring forth," thus whatever you feed yourself is what you will eventually consciously, unconsciously, or subconsciously share with the world.

We also need to have a comprehensive knowledge of our cultural heritage. The phrase that "there is nothing new under the sun" can be applied to how we analyze our history. It carries with it revelations about what is encoded in our very DNA. A titanic figure in the early part of the 20th century and giant among men of his day, Marcus Mosiah Garvey, wrote this about one's personal and cultural history, "A people without knowledge of their history, origin and culture is like a tree without roots." For this reason, we should take interest and be critical about what any teacher instructs about your cultural history. This has profound implications for minorities, particularly Black people, in American society because there are consistent distortions of the truth, yet it is fed to young minds and accepted as truth. Never be afraid to ask for the source of facts when you feel that an opinion speaks negatively against you. For this reason, among others, there should be a proactive and operational definition of education. If you define education by others' standards, then you will only seek but so much.

There is but one more powerful thing left to discuss within education and that is the fact that education is not as small as something that can only be learned but also experienced. The 19th century writer and poet Oscar Wilde offers this thought, "Education is an admirable thing, but it is well to remember from time to time that nothing that is worth knowing can be taught."

There is another adage that couples with this and that is

commonly stated which is "experience is the best teacher." It is appropriate to discard the belief that every occurrence that happens in your life is not a part of the learning continuum. Each morning that your eyes open is a new opportunity to learn through the day's happenings for the truth is that you have never experienced that day before. You may go to the same job, hang with identical friends, eat familiar foods, but you have never felt or experienced that new day. Appreciate each one and what it must offer you.

This is the principal difference between knowledge and education because there are infinite sources of the latter. Only through education can you develop your mental prowess enough to be known as a wise person. Confucius, the brilliant thinker whose thoughts were converted into a religion, wrote, "By three methods we can learn wisdom: First, by reflection, which is noblest; second, by imitation, which is the easiest; and third by experience, which is the bitterest." This highlights the complexity that comes with moving through the cycles of your educational journey.

It is not necessary to go over these in length for we will later, but it is critical to mention that you must be willing to do all three to save yourself time and energy. As long as you are operating with hope and you want to progress in life, you will need to reflect on whatever happens in your life.

Also, you will save yourself a great deal of time by not repeating the mistakes of those who have come before you. Lastly, it is through experience that you will be dealt blows in your life but it is a necessary evil for growth and to develop wisdom. These three simple things are how you will be able to activate the knowledge you consume and customize your education so that it is always to your life's benefit. Education is and always will be what you make it. Accept this and move forward aggressively.

Time

Have you ever wondered what would happen if you unplugged from the world for just one month? This would include no TV, no cell phone, no social media, and no outside interference outside from your assigned schedule. The effects would be undeniable and probably long-lasting in terms of your perception of what is happening around you. An even scarier question, what would you do if you were left alone with nothing to distract you? Do you live with enough purpose for this time to be spent moving your life aggressively forward? A more menacing question for some may be to simply look in the mirror, then wonder whether you love the person you see enough to spend that much time alone with him/her? Furthermore, do you value that person's opinions and always do what is in his/her most positive interest?

These questions have profound implications on the mind of a dreamer with a restless spirit or brings shame to a stagnant soul who has allowed time to diminish their once bright future. They force such people to look inward to better comprehend their inner desire that calls them to aspire to go higher in every aspect of life.

"In all our deeds, the proper value and respect for time determines success or failure," a quote from the infamous and brilliant Malcolm X. This highlights the importance of placing value on one's time and how it can determine your future positively or negatively. Charles Darwin, father of the theory of evolution, stated, "A man who dares to waste one hour of time has not discovered the value of life," which simply drives the point that every moment is precious.

Time will be defined as "an appointed, fit, due, or proper instant or period with reference to personal experience of a specified kind." Why this definition? Because it forces you to feel a sense of obligation about how you spend your time as well as the fact that it has a definite endpoint. For all those people on the sidelines of life waiting patiently for the right moment, right job, or right circumstance, please keep in mind that no one lives forever.

Is it not highly ironic that from the moment you are born you are moving closer to death? That may be starling to think about it but death is inevitable and you are not invincible, regardless of how fast, strong, wise, or good looking you may be.

Therefore, your time is the most important commodity that you can ever possess because it can never be stored or stockpiled. With that newfound understanding, how would you better protect yours? Would you consume more knowledge? Remove a bad habit? Become more health conscious? It should be spent doing something that will improve the condition of your life or in service to some higher calling aka your purpose.

Think about the new trend in television of "reality" shows. The premise requires that you, the viewer, sit down and watch other people act out scripted roles on camera and the crazy part is that they convince the masses that it is their truth. What if you spent that time constructing your own reality? Whatever changes must be made, I would suggest strongly pursuing them with aggression.

I am asking that you remove unnecessary distractions from your life and simply be intentional about what you allow to influence your psyche and the way you spend each moment of your existence. The hard truth is that every person on Earth has the same 24-hours to utilize to move their lives progressively forward; how they are spent makes the difference to whether you are the one watching "reality" or living it.

Now to address the notion of duty, a concept that has deceived millions for years on end. Everyone at some point has felt that they are bound by duty in the support of another individual or strong beliefs in their life. This can be a major drain on your time and provide a seemingly foolproof excuse for why you mismanage your day, week, month, or entire life. Do not get me wrong, we all have circumstances that cause us to stray from our plans but if this is consistent then the problem is you. If you are not willing to be accountable for the management of your time than other people will never be comfortable investing theirs with you. Morehouse has a long-standing saying, "To be early is to be on-time, to be on-time is to be late, and to be late is unacceptable." I thought it was just another adage that had no serious importance to the progression of my life until I got into the corporate world and it began shaping the perception my bosses had of me. It is sadly true that "time is of the essence," and it comes at a premium because it is the only thing you can never recover.

For this very reason, we must confront one of the worst

habits to have: Procrastination. As before, I want to be clear on how we are defining it especially because it has been such a monumental hindrance to the productivity of so many, including myself. What I found was "the act or habit of putting off or delaying, especially something requiring immediate attention." Thus, by engaging in procrastination, by definition, is the admission that you accept three terribly problematic things.

First, it obviously shows that you do not value the time you should complete a task. Having the task itself implies that you have already accepted responsibility, willingly or otherwise, to complete the task. Without the completion of the task, chances are that there was some type of negative outcome that comes your way, even one that you cannot see initially. For example, when a teacher would assign homework that you did not complete, it was not a big deal and was often overlooked, but when you missed the information for the test then you felt the effects. Life is much the same because whatever you refuse to accept responsibility for will likely come back around. We often do not see the value or growth in an opportunity until it has long passed.

Secondly, we should understand that every opportunity worth something in life has an expiration date. The meaning of procrastination highlights that something needed "immediate attention." Thus, we only have a specified time to make good on all our potential to do something worthwhile. No person successful ever waited for anything to come to him/her, but rather went after it. Remember that our world has been sped up tremendously over the last 10-15 years, which has contributed to diminishing the lifespan of any opportunity. If you do not accept the job, how hard is it to find someone to replace you nowadays? Therefore, you need to have intentionality about seizing the chance to take center stage.

Lastly, we should highlight that there is a serious lack in sense of urgency among procrastinators. The overused statement that "time waits for no man" still reigns true, but it is even more pressing now than ever before. Leonardo Da Vinci wrote, "I have been impressed with the urgency of doing. Knowing is not enough, we must apply," which is incredibly appropriate to the ambitious or stagnant person who wants change to be possible for their situation.

Purpose

It has become common practice that guidance counselors and other trusted advisors tell you to "find your passion" and "chase your dreams," but rarely does it come with any additional perspective on how to do so. Yet, we encounter so many things that interest us over the years, it is also extremely difficult to narrow down your choices.

At some point, you can be sure to hear that you should "do whatever makes you happy" and the infamous "whatever you would do for free is your passion." The craziest thing to consider is what if all of them are correct? How hard (or easy) would your choice be if you accepted all of them? We would potentially have a serious issue on our hands, but there is certain simplicity present in asking the question, "What is your purpose?" Here is how.

Purpose has a laundry list of synonyms that should reveal

much about how it is should inform your decisions. Some of the most prominent, and only ones we will consider, are: aim, ambition, desire, direction, function, goal, objective, plan, premeditation, reason, target, and will. These were the words chosen because each of these words has a finite end, which presupposes a start date. All of them place a demand on something that is very deliberate or focused. It is important to look at purpose in this way for it is such a vast concept with seemingly infinite possibilities. However, there was a reason that purpose was the final area slated for deconstruction.

It is important that you have a renewed perception of knowledge, conscience, education, and a newfound respect for time before trying to tackle who you are to be in the world. No man or woman is exempt from reconciling their constructed thoughts of their past and present with their desired future.

The automobile magnate Henry Ford uttered these words, "Coming together is a beginning; keeping together is progress; working together is success," which speaks volumes for the lens that will allow you to understand your purpose with clarity. Steve Jobs had a fascinating point of view on this topic that speaks to what is necessary to find your purpose that he used in his everyday life, "That's been one of my mantras –focus and simplicity. Simple can be harder than complex: You must work hard to get your thinking clean to make it simple. But it is worth it in the end because once you get there, you can move mountains."

It is painstaking work to get to the root of what brings you the most joy, especially when you should consider what to do to sustain yourself and your loved ones. It is not an easy choice to make but this is when you must trust in your own ability and capacity for growth. For this book, we will address the search for purpose through three of the synonyms which are: desire, function, and premeditation. First, there must be a unification of passion and purpose that can be applicable to one's life.

Passion is the driving force behind your innermost desire to do something that you love that you cannot see yourself living without. If you are so fortunate to be able to pay your bills by executing your passion than you are already ahead of the game. For all the rest of the world, we must deal with the harsh reality that we cannot only operate by doing solely what we love.

Your passion can also be considered your craft. It is the set of skills that you do for fun, utilize as an escape from reality, and develop because it brings you joy. This is something that also has the opportunity to become the way you consistently educate yourself. Within your passion you should make a home for your wildest and most lavish dreams because without it you will never achieve them.

The television and philanthropic giant, Oprah Winfrey, offers this: "Passion is energy. Feel the power that comes from focusing on what excited you." Only through your passion you will be able to find your purpose because it is the only thing that will set your soul ablaze. Famed theologian and philosopher Howard Thurman wrote this about these phenomena, "Don't ask what the world needs. Ask what makes you come alive, and go do it. Because what the world needs is people who have come alive."

Purpose has much more to do with functionality than

anything else though it is saturated with passion. A function is "the kind of action or activity proper to a person, thing, or institution," which makes it clear that it carries the burden of appropriateness. This should blow your mind because it suggests that there is a proper and improper way to go about seeking purpose. Therefore, we should be considerate of the fact that there is a natural process to understanding the functional or operational development of your purpose.

Please do not assume that this is somehow pigeon holed into a certain method, because that could not be the furthest thing from the truth. It means that there must be an intentional act that is appropriately suited for the person whom delivers it. Frankly, it calls for a service something that is original to the person executing the work. To truly be operating within your purpose your function should have a quality of service that helps someone outside of yourself. It is through that service that your function will steer your passion and open opportunity to share your body of work with the world.

One of my favorite quotes is from one of the preeminent theologians, educators, and divinely-inspired men of the 20th century, the sixth president of Morehouse College, Dr. Benjamin Elijah Mays, mentor to Dr. Martin Luther King Jr., when he states," Every man and woman is born into the world to do something unique and distinctive and if he or she does not do it, it will never be done." This perfectly captures the idea of purpose as it highlights that you have a specific *do*, a planned course of action.

The last component for the full working definition of purpose is premeditation. It means that it was specific and focused and consequently "on purpose." This is relatively self-explanatory as it means that there was a plan in place.

I feel it appropriate to highlight one of my favorite lines from B-list celebrity and Jay-Z protégé, J. Cole, when he rhymed, "You hated and I levitated further, knew I would kill the game premeditated murder." It drives the point home that he believed in himself and his ability so much that he set a plan in place to accomplish his goals. Another example is with Muhammad Ali who earnestly proclaimed himself the greatest before he was or LeBron James who called himself "King" before he even hit the pros. But you also should take note of the pressure they put on themselves to earn those names. Anytime you have a goal there is an increased measure of accountability that cannot be overlooked. There is a greater sense that you have a responsibility to fulfill whatever you set out to achieve.

Have you ever considered why premeditation or conspiracy is a crime more harshly punished? It is because it took so much forethought and contemplation that it should carry a harsher penalty. Deliberation led to successful execution. You must do the same for your purpose.

The final working definition we have is *"a sustainable, deliberate desire to perform a specific act of service that drives a person to develop self."* It encompasses all the aspects but focuses on the adaptations that are necessary to translate into something that will last over an extended period.

Lastly, your purpose is about the definitive body of work that it produces. With this newfound insight, you can ensure that it happens properly. If you work hard at any purpose for long enough it will begin to become part of your everyday life and your very identity. This work that is done consistently and passionately will help with the establishment of a legacy that can be left behind after you move on or when it is your time to leave this earth. It has always been essential as I traveled through my everyday life to ensure that it was purpose-filled. That is the way you leave a legacy that those who come behind you can build upon.

The entire purpose in opening the book this way was to set the table for the rest of the book as you read. I wanted to give a sound understanding of my beliefs but more importantly to establish that I am as human as you. As you read on, there are even more stories that I will share and that give insight to the type of person I am. Is there a clear-cut prescription or method that you will learn from this book? Absolutely but I did not want to share wisdom that is seemingly unattainable.

I never wanted to take for granted what blessings I was bestowed and how that impacted my outlook on life. I wanted to make a point to share myself as I wrote each paragraph which is the principle reason this book has taken so long to write.

I was not the man I needed to be when I came up with the concept for this book over five years ago. The reality is that I bared my soul in every chapter, yet I lacked the necessary character to serve you, the reader, the best way possible. Recognizing this was half the battle. Being man enough to sit on it was another struggle, but it helped me develop into a true wellspring of guidance for you.

Years ago, I was asked about the dominating skill that I possessed and how it manifest itself in my everyday life. As I sat and pondered on this question for a couple minutes it finally dawned on me what unique talent I had. The talent was to create mutually beneficial situations for everyone who came into my life personally or professionally. I am not heavily into astrology but I attribute this to being a Libra, the scale, which also symbolizes justice and balance. Also on several subsequent character strengths assessments it has been determined that judgment and fairness are some of my stronger strengths. Thus, there is rarely a situation where I feel that I have taken advantage of another person or done something that negatively impacts another being. This is the same notion that caused me to hold onto this manuscript for so long and postpone its release on multiple occasions. If you provide a blessing to me through your purchase of this text then I felt that every chapter, every paragraph, and every word was worth more than what you paid. Call me old-fashioned but I believe I owe that to you.

So, as you read on, make sure that you get the most out of each concept by reading it while taking notes; trust there are plenty of takeaways. But let us hypothetically say you get nothing at all from the book then I leave you with the classic words of Andre 3000 when he said, "I swear it don't cost much, to pay attention to me. I tell it how it is and I tell it how it could be." If this book does nothing for you, then give it away to another being who may have a shackled rebel soul.

Necessity for the Rebel

"What is a rebel? A man who says no: but whose refusal does not imply a renunciation."

-Albert Camus

America has always embraced the rebel. Our history as a country is filled with stories of some of its greatest people (inventors, political figures, musicians, activists, academics, etc.) who challenged the way things were. There has always been someone ready to take on the power structure to mandate a change or to conquer the great unknown. America, and societies worldwide in general, have never been willing to accept change without some sort of demand from those who are subject to its rule.

History gives a long list of those people who have fought and in some cases, were willing to die for that much-needed change. This willingness to demand change is the hallmark of every great American who has ever done more than maintain or serve the status quo. Our greatest Americans who are always thrust in front of us as key figures to be celebrated were some of the fiercest opponents to the words, "that's just the way things are."

Some of my personal favorite rebels are names like John Hanson, Frederick Douglass, Denmark Vesey, Nat Turner, Booker T. Washington, W.E.B. Dubois, John Hope, Howard Thurman, Benjamin Elijah Mays, Ella Baker, Martin Luther King, Jr., Malcolm X, James Baldwin, Maynard Jackson, Marian Wright Edelman and all the way to Shawn "Jay-Z" Carter, Kendrick Lamar, J. Cole and President Barack Obama.

Some of these names may sound foreign to you but

consequently they are all in some large or small part my personal heroes but they are names we should all embrace for one reason or another.

Before we get too deep into who these people were we must better understand what they represented, which simply put is progress. They were all people who believed that the way things were was not the way things should remain in the future. They were all dreamers, all optimists, all driven passionately by their stark opposition to the status quo. More importantly they identified with a cause that was greater than themselves and worked feverishly towards it. These people were not simply chasing money or trying to provide only themselves more luxuries, but rather found space in their hearts (and conscience) to include the masses; repercussions be damned.

Their own personal well-being, physically, spiritually, emotionally, etc., were sacrificed for the betterment of society. It was their passion that woke them up each morning and their desire to create change that made them stand out from the crowd. This passion or fire burning in their souls could never be dimmed and no amount of opposition to their struggle was enough to cause them to stop. They were resilient. Quitting was never an option. Goals were set and accomplished time and again until change was realized. They operated in excellence regardless of what stood against them.

"No" was not an answer that was accepted nor tolerated. It was never a deterrent for these people because whenever someone said it they understood that it simply meant "not yet." So, the next day they would start all over again with hope in believing that today will be that glorious day when "yes" was the response. This is the exact temperament that everyone has with the financial aid office at an HBCU (inside joke). Much like any good salesman they would go person to person selling their product which in their case is wisdom and hope. They remained optimistic, though there were moments when defeat felt worse than death, enough to always start the next day to start the fight again. They were persistent.

No matter what they were faced with they kept their eyes on the prize of a better tomorrow. If they had breath in their lungs there was nothing whatsoever that could deter their will to win. In the eternal words of Vince Lombardi, "Winners never quit and quitters never win." Most of the people who do not succeed are the ones who stopped trying too soon; these were not those people. They saw their rebellion or discontent with the status quo as their method to love the world.

It was with this love, which many at the time called "misguided," they were able to impact the lives of millions of people. This love manifested itself through acts of service on behalf of society wholesale.

One of them, Marian Wright Edelman, my heroine, wrote about this saying, "Service is the rent we pay for living." These people were leaders who understood that their challenge to the status quo dictated their allegiance to the service of other people. They were unyielding servants.

The explanation of the characteristics of these people is paramount in understanding the nature of the rebel. The cause that you serve, the passion that drives your every breath (or should) is what is mission critical for you to transcend. Transcend what? Transcend the limitations that society has placed on you due to factors outside of your control. What are these factors? The family you're born into, the color of your skin, whether you are man or woman, the amount of money your parents have, what period you are born in, etc. We all acquire preconditions that are 100% not our doing but are 100% our responsibility to acknowledge, negotiate, and at times overcome. These are the facts of life.

Clear as Night & Day

No matter what I do, I will wake up tomorrow as a Black man. That comes with certain liabilities that other men of different races do not have to deal with. It may not be fair and it may not be politically or morally correct but I cannot concern myself with things that are simply facts.

Here is the reality, I cannot change what is in my DNA or that I am a descendant of people who were enslaved throughout the Western Hemisphere or even that I started balding at 23; they are just facts. Facts that I do not have time to wrestle with or complain about or ask God why this happened to me. Facts are concrete, finite and are resolute. Every minute you waste challenging facts is a minute you cannot use to create new ones. Message!

Have you ever dreamed of being in a better place? One that was more blissful and serene with no problems and no unnecessary drama? WAKE UP! This is not Disney and there is no prince coming to save you on a magic horse or fairy godmother flying around to make your road easier. If you are fortunate to live a life without immense strain or strife, then you are one of the privileged few. For the rest of us, life is entirely what we make of it and we limit what we can make of it by fighting unnecessary battles. On the contrary, you have a mandate to fight without cease against whatever stands in the way of your progress including yourself. Tupac Shakur once asked, "Is it a crime, to fight, for what is mine?" The safe answer is hell to the no.

No matter what I do, I will wake up tomorrow as a Black man. (Just thought I would reiterate this fact.) That means that in America I am held to an entirely different standard than everyone else.

Each morning I have no choice but to defy the stereotypes that society has prescribed to those who look like me. Every local news station in the country depicts Black men in a negative light by primarily highlighting criminal activity. In the 2012 report *Mainstream Representations of Young Black Men and Boys* revealed that "close to seven in 10 stories of black young men and boys related in some form to crime" on the news with a focus on "murder involving knives and/or gangs." Regardless if you agree with these views or perceptions they form a stereotype, *a widely held but fixed and* <u>*oversimplified*</u> *image or idea of a particular type of person or thing*, that I have the burden to disprove.

I operate under the belief that I am perceived guilty and I must fight to prove my innocence or better still transcendence. My skin in conjunction with my gender make me the most feared human being on this planet because of what the mainstream media/society has defined as my innate characteristics; those characteristics are violent, irrational, and emotionally volatile.

Emory University in Atlanta, GA has one of the most beautiful campuses in America and has a melting pot of ethnicities and cultures who study on their campus. With nearly 15,000 students and widely considered to be a "Southern Ivy," Emory is one of the best institutions in the country.

Emory also has the largest library in Atlanta thanks to the generosity of Robert W. Woodruff, who donated three libraries to different institutions throughout the city. So as a history major who was constantly doing research I had a fond appreciation for their collection. It became painfully obvious that Black men were the most feared human beings in America one night as I traveled on their campus. It was common for students from around the city to visit each other's libraries as they all shared the same nickname "Woody" and access.

So, I arrived at Emory late, which was my custom because I was so active all afternoon and evening, but that day I had a full suit on. As I walked from the parking garage to front door, I watched two groups of women, one white and one Asian, cross the street as I approached. Immediately I thought, "I have a suit on and a book bag. What could be intimidating about me?" Only thing left to attribute it to was my skin. Some might say "it was late" or "you're a man and they're women" or any number of excuses to justify the reason behind their unwarranted fear; they are all poor excuses masking the truth. The reality is that no matter what I wear, how I speak, my income, how cultured I am, etc. I will always be held with equivalent contempt (on sight) commensurate to what the media portrays.

My Black skin affords certain liabilities that must always be accounted for as I navigate life. A liability, by definition, is simply "something disadvantageous" with synonyms as follows: accountability, burden, debt, duty, and obligation. So, the unfortunate but very real reality that being a Black male in America brings is that I carry the burden of a litany of stereotypes that I must surpass. These stereotypes that are consistently perpetuated from biases in the minds of whoever willingly accept them to be true which creates prejudice. This prejudice over time evolves into discrimination when it subtly begins to influence policy and lawmakers who oversee institutions that are designed to serve all people. When these discriminatory policies are in place for an extended period, they create *de jure* systems designed to institutionalize racism. A perfect example of this comes within the criminal justice system which has come under great scrutiny in the past few years. Here's some facts for you...There are 1 in 3 chances as a Black man that I will spend time in prison in my lifetime where 1 in 15 Black men are currently in prison. That means that Black men are nearly 40% of the entire prison population yet we are only 15.2% of the U.S. population. This compares to 1 in 106 white men currently in prison who represent 32.1% of the prison population. But wait there's more...white men represent 31% of the population (very proportionate wouldn't you say?). Long story short, there is a great disparity in the way that the criminal justice system applies justice; this is one liability that comes with being a black male in America. No matter what the scenario I will never feel comfortable in two situations regardless if I am right or wrong. These two scenarios are: 1) being pulled over by police and 2) standing in front of a judge. History suggests that I am more likely to be treated less than fairly in those situations. This is an undeniable fact.

It seems like every night on the news there is another killing of a Black male somewhere in the country. It is an unfortunate reality that must be accounted for each and every time that I have an encounter with police. Have I ever been arrested? No. Does this change the fact that there are evident and deep-rooted issues with the discrimination in police forces? Not at all. Have I ever been racially profiled? More times than I can count. For most people that does not make a difference to how they operate in their everyday life, but for us it is a raw reality we must face and be proactive to combat. But does money protect me from this? Ask Henry Louis Gates, famed Harvard professor, did it help him even on his property. For no reason other than my or his or any Black males' skin does it make us more susceptible to this kind of repression. But guess what happens now that I know about it? Nothing externally without hard work and consistent pressure on legislators but I still have the personal responsibility to limit its impact on my life. No reason to allow it to be a deterrent or an excuse to why I cannot progress in this country.

I should note that though this is not serious opposition to me, a college-educated young professional, but I understand that it is a treacherous liability for many who look like me. My education is my privilege and key determinant to being able to evade the clutches of the criminal justice system because of the luxuries it affords me. Not everyone is so fortunate because once you are in the criminal justice system you can never leave it behind you as a Black man. It strips you of your ability to make a reasonable or sound living barring you from employment and increasing your opportunity for recidivism. A Black man in America who has a criminal record is placed in the worst possible situation to succeed in America. For example, in national employment reporting by the U.S. Department of Labor it shows that a white male with a criminal record is more likely to be employed than his Black counterpart with no criminal history.

It was not so much that I was worried or concerned with my future opportunities or lack thereof because of my behavior but I knew that it could alter my most formative years as an adult. The years between 18-23 are by far the most stimulating and most dangerous you live as a young adult. For me, a Black male, they are the make or break time on whether I will be able to defy the odds or become a statistic.

Honestly, the reason I decided to write this book was because I realized making it across the stage during my college graduation that I was a rebel in American society. Not just because I graduated but because I was blessed to had never been arrested, my work was going to influence the lives of thousands of youth nationwide, and I was fortunate enough escape my circumstances when so many others were not able.

Many people trivialize the struggle, for who Jesus would call, "the least of these," in America which are Black males unfortunately. To put all of this in perspective here are some stats for you: 1 in 2

Black males will see the inside of a prison before age 23, only 1 in 3 Black males graduates from college nationally. Only 45% of Black males graduate HS in my hometown of Cincinnati and this figure only stands at 59% nationally compared to 80% for our white counterparts. These statistics came from the Bureau of Justice Statistics, and frankly I trust them.

Given the academic, criminal justice, and economic barriers (to name a few) that Black males must overcome to attain success, it is more than a blessing but a miracle to see the glorious spectacle which is a Morehouse College graduation. Shamefully, it is the only place in the world where 500 men of African-descent graduate annually with Bachelor's degrees. To share that experience with Elijah, who was three years old at the time, was such an epic occasion and by far the most important moment in his life for him to see.

More than A House

When finding real life examples of those who embodied what it meant to be a rebel I must think about my First 48 experience. It was not simply the fact that I graduated from college, but it was the way I got it done. In the first 48 hours of being at Morehouse during New Student Orientation, I found out that my high school sweetheart and recent ex-girlfriend was pregnant. I literally got out of line headed into "Welcome to the House" to field the call and got the devastating news.

Remember this was even before my father left to return to Cincinnati. When he left he said simply this:" You know what to do.

You know what name you represent. I'll be back in four years." He did not set foot back in Atlanta until my graduation. Thanks Pops for the vote of confidence! I needed that.

I was never more excited or nervous in my life because I had, for the first time in my life, become a statistic. The very thing I fought so hard for, getting out of Cincinnati, was about to be stripped from me. All the sacrificing and all the self-discipline would be wasted because of one misguided evening of passion. I thought I had only one semester to enjoy Atlanta and I would be transferring back to University of Cincinnati (my safety school).

As you already know, I did not leave Morehouse but what you did not know is the enormity of the struggle I overcame to make it across that glorious stage on the Green at 8am (rain or shine). I will be sharing more as we go along but I had to highlight that I too had to overcome self-doubt in a major way. It is a major key to progress. I doubted everything in that time of my life. I doubted if I was meant to be there or if I had the capacity to be a good father at such a young age. Doubt if I would be able to balance grades, campus life, and fatherhood. Reservations if I had enough drive, passion, and desire to overcome this newfound obstacle in my life. When it all came down to it there were a few things that I refused to let go: 1) my mission in life was to become an educator who would change thousands of lives; 2) being raised by a single father, I would be active in my child's life or die trying; 3) I could do more for him by graduating from Morehouse than anywhere else. These three things later coupled with the loss of my ill grandfather on Dec. 18, 2007, which happened to be the day after

I told my father and grandmother about the impending grandson, changed me. It fueled my every waking moment. Before leaving his deathbed, I promised him two things that have driven me daily which were, "I will change the world of education and I will raise that boy right." I still avidly refuse to be made out to be a liar thus I work still to fulfill my promise. Accepting "no" has never been an option for me over the years nor will it ever be.

Every time I think back to those amazing, treacherous, enriching, tiring, passionate, struggle-filled, divinely-inspired, and mesmerizing years I spent in college, I am in utter disbelief at what I was able to accomplish. Freshman year I was my dorm's vice president and was active in campus politics and community volunteerism. Elijah Mitchell Collins came into the world during finals week to the great surprise of many people.

All first semester I dealt with it in silence until Thanksgiving break when I could no longer hide my distress and close friends became deeply concerned with my behavior. Still only a privileged few were in the loop of what was happening in my life so it still shocked the world with his arrival.

On April 28, 2008 mid-afternoon, Elijah came into the world and life never was the same. Much to the chagrin of Elijah's mother and much to my father's delight, I stayed at Morehouse. It was an instant dose of reality and seemingly never-ending saga as I became seemingly more acquainted with highways than hallways and more familiar with mileage than pre-calculus literally.

For the next four years, I made at least 50 trips back and forth to Cincinnati to ensure that I was always an integral part of his life including every break. It was always an adventure to make it back for class late Sunday night, but still a worthwhile journey and sacrifice every time.

Everyone knew me as the foremost champion of education on campus who was always willing to take on administration. The cause? Getting more Black men into classrooms nationwide and Morehouse was the perfect place for this mission. I started Morehouse Education Association, the first organization of its kind, and recruited for teaching organizations from around the U.S. I had attained a certain level of notoriety for this work but nothing brought me more attention than when Elijah came to campus.

See Elijah aka Eli was something like a rock star because so many people had seen him via Facebook (and he worked his dimples so well). So, when he finally was old enough, he would go to class with daddy and we'd run through Spelman and Clark Atlanta for kicks. All I can say is that the boy was lethal with the ladies which I never had a problem with of course.

Long story short, Eli diametrically changed my life from the tender age of 19 to live my life in way that I would become so much more than I ever imagined. Why? Because I figured that he would never be served effectively by me dreaming small or succumbing to "being realistic." I knew I had a mandate to never stop growing and never stop moving forward regardless of what I had to personally sacrifice.

Life became an obstacle course that I had to see to the other side. We already know that the odds were stacked against me to make it out of college period. So, I made the decision to not be stopped by anything or anyone. Sleep did not matter nor food nor feelings at all but rather I was so deeply immersed in fulfilling my promises that nothing mattered. Not saying there were not times where the struggle got so bad that I could not see straight but I knew that I would make it over. I cried in disappointment, I fought to survive, I hustled and worked odd jobs to provide for Eli, I crashed on more couches and floors than you can imagine, but I made it. For example, the first half of junior year I had one pair of jeans, one pair of shoes without holes in the bottom, one suit (stains included), no financial aid, 20 hours per semester, five executive boards I worked on, weekly community service, 2 part-time jobs, 80 in-school observation hours in Atlanta Public Schools, contracted bronchitis, and when I could afford it I travelled back to Cincinnati to see little man. All I can say about this time in my life is to share what one of my mentors in HS told me, "if you don't know God now, you'll get to know Him in college." Nothing ever reigned truer than those words but none of it would have been possible without Him or them, my brothers at The House. Forever grateful to the brotherhood for we truly were each other's strength and solace when times were rough; none of us at Morehouse graduate alone, we do it together. *Et facta est lux.*

      If you were to ask an average person on the street would I have been able to graduate, they would emphatically tell you that I would not. Stereotypical behavior alone would dictate that I was not going to graduate at all or that I would have been a deadbeat dad. Nothing but individual determination made the difference to whether I would defy the odds. Some say it would have made more sense to do something easier or it would have been more convenient, which I cannot disagree.

The difference is that it would not have been worth as much as it is now. The experience alone molded me into an amazingly resilient and deeply spiritual young man who knows beyond a shadow of a doubt that no mountain is too high to climb and no valley too deep to cross. Morehouse taught me something about myself that is priceless about what I have inside of me if I simply focus and dedicate myself to a mission. This is my drawn-out way of saying that anything can be achieved if you refuse to believe what others say about you or believe you cannot succeed. It is a matter of pushing yourself to limits unknown and striving for things that at times seem unattainable with unwavering faith in God and oneself. This is the untold story of America and what can be achieved when you focus your time and energies into the right stuff. Better still, it is the story of the subculture of American society among Black males, the one that is rarely acknowledged or that makes the news.

It was critical to share this with you because you can never overlook or underestimate the importance of the times when you made a conscious decision to accomplish a goal and saw it to the end. Why is that so important? Because no man or woman has ever impacted the world without first being able to master self-doubt. For Black males and minorities in general, we have a unique challenge to define success for ourselves culturally and socially. At any point, we can view ourselves through the lens of dominant culture but there will always be a serious deficit in that approach.

Only on rare occasions does one find positive imagery of

themselves in dominant culture that are purely organic and value every facet of what makes them wonderfully made. There has always been an underlying message that beauty and progress is prescribed to those who look a certain way or act following a certain set of rules. It is the history of minority groups in America and abroad that they are kept socially oppressed for as long as humanly possible which is evidenced in debates over economic disparities, access to social mobility, citizenship vs. deportation, and even with "inalienable" rights such as voting and the application of justice.

This bastion, this flagship institution on the forefront of social justice for the Black male worldwide has been an essential part of my manifestation as a man. The conscious decision to stay at Morehouse is and always will be the best decision ever made because it changed how I thought about the world and what I thought possible of myself.

This book, these very words were birthed at Mother Morehouse because I walked the hallowed grounds that many a giant walked before me. It was on those red clay hills in Georgia that I learned to lead and more importantly learned to serve wholeheartedly. I had etched on my soul that "Knowledge plus character -- that is the true goal of education," a quote from my beloved brother Martin King, Jr. '48. It was where I devoured and became full on quotes from Bro. Howard Thurman '23 such as, "What happens to you cannot defeat you unless you allow it to get in you." (It is so poignant I figured I would us it twice.) I was submerged in a world of profound thoughts and inspiration while surrounded by other men who not only shared my pigment but also my passion to change the world.

Many pundits argue the merits or necessity of Historically Black Colleges and Universities, yet in a time such as this they are more needed than ever. There is a restlessness among people that demands a change in the methodology subscribed to by American society. The raw reality of persistent deprivation and repression has made our society ripe for aggressive and divisive revolt against these systems. According to the U.S. Constitution, it is our birthright and duty as American citizens to do so.

Given this burgeoning reality, there will be even more need for affluent, ambitious young Black professionals to drive social change in a positive manner. Not saying that these people will come from HBCUs, but the reality is that per capita we produce more highly-skilled Black professionals than from anywhere else. The curricula, which at minimum broaches the subject of social justice and industrial equity, is one that can ever be discounted in the climate we are in presently. Even as you consider the movement of Black Lives Matter it is important to realize that tangible, sustainable change is something that will have to be designed with deep input from those it will serve. Those scholars, lawyers, economists, historians, doctors, and theorists will have to come from some institution of higher education for it to be widely adopted; simply the rules of the game. Who's more apt than a graduate of a HBCU?

A Rebel's Playground

We, African-Americans, have had a long road to secure any progress and a perilous fight with the dominant culture to level the playing field. It produces a culture of "haves" and "have nots" that has created the greatest wealth disparity in the history of the world. Where 84% of wealth in America is controlled by the top 20% and the bottom 40% possess 0.3% of it, according to *The Atlantic.*

We live in a society that has made the conscious, money-motivated decision toward mass incarceration of its citizens where we are 3% of the world's population but have 25% of its prison population, according to Department of Justice. Furthermore, Huffington Post reports some 60% of the prison population is people of color though we make up 30% of the U.S. population. On top of that, we live in a country where the Black unemployment rate was 10.6% in February 2015 compared to 4.7% to our white counterparts.

Systemic equality is a myth in America and it is the lens that I must view the world through not because I want to, but because it was forced upon me. Let us be real in this moment folks, no race of people (as a whole) would choose to find themselves on the bottom of every positive statistical category and at the top of every negative one. There are systems in place that maintain the status quo which protect the "haves" and alienate then subjugate the "have-nots." We must come to the realization that this is our society regardless of how much we want it to be different or have optimism that tomorrow will be different. We must work to change it but we must accept it for what it is.

The reason this is so important to you, the reader/listener, and me, the writer/storyteller is that we should be able to accept the truth that other people share. If everyone could live the Disney life, we would without hesitation. So, do not take for granted the beauty others glean from your life.

If we all could have the stereotypical upbringing with two parents, a six-figure household, an amazing private school education from preschool through college, annual travels around the world, and exposure to fine arts and cultures outside of our own, we most definitely would. It comes from a place of immense privilege to be able to disregard the experience of those who have had a different, less convenient upbringing as you may have had.

Privilege is another one of those words that must be completely unpacked before we can make strides to not see it as a detrimental or derogatory term aimed at those more fortunate. Privilege, by definition, is "*a special right, immunity, or exemption granted to persons in authority to free them from certain obligations or liabilities.*" The keys to this definition are three-fold: special immunity granted, persons in authority, and free from liabilities. Each of these tells a story all its own about the realities that privilege allows.

First, it is a "special immunity" which already specifies that this is something that not everyone has access to. When my mother was pregnant with my brother she contracted chicken pox, which meant that my brother could not get them during childhood. It was three to four kids who caught it all at the same time. Thanks to my little cousin Brandon who decided to share the wealth. But the amazing thing was my brother was immune to it, because my mother had chicken pox while pregnant with him, and he never had to deal with it; it was his special immunity, though he did nothing to earn it.

To quote Warren Buffett who spoke to this, "if I had been born Black or female I would not have been afforded the same opportunities that I had as a white male." Also, it says that it was "granted" which assumes that it was not something that had to be fought for or a struggle to possess. It is something that is bestowed upon someone. That does not mean that that person should be ashamed of that fact though. No matter what we feel about how the chips fell it was outside of our control and it shaped our reality. All facts, no feelings.

Next, we come to our second grouping of words which is often the most overlooked and underappreciated part of privilege. When we discuss "persons in authority" in the context of privilege, it also is double entendre for discrimination which is also a point of much contention. I figured we might as well broach the subject now because it has shaped our society in very real ways. It is through persons in authority that there have been distinct and deeply bigoted policies, laws and entire systems within local, state, and national government that have caused some of the realities that minorities in America must overcome to attain any measure of success. Lord Acton said it best when he wrote, "Power tends to corrupt and absolute power corrupts absolutely."

The statistics are all factual examples that there is something else at play then the stereotypical, racist narrative that "everyone can pull themselves up by their bootstraps if they work hard enough." Let's be real, that is the greatest lie ever told from generation after generation because those persons in power have always maintained much of the status quo to ensure their own gains (which should be expected). Position and power are unfortunately something that minorities in this country have not had the opportunity to possess for any considerable amount of time or on any great scale. Persons in authority, historically, have always and primarily meant white Anglo-Saxon Protestant (WASP) males in American society. All facts, no feelings.

Lastly, we must come to grips with "free from liabilities" and what it presumes. It offers us this truth in understanding that those with privilege carry less burdens than those without it. A liability is one less thing to have to consider in your journey toward a successful life. If you lived without having to wonder how the rent would be paid or where your next meal comes from then more power to you, but it is not the reality for most people who must navigate the world. No matter the struggle or strife others face, we cannot impose our privilege on those who are less fortunate. Big KRIT, one of the best Southern lyricists in hip-hop, painted this picture beautifully when he said, "Put yourself in my shoes, if you had no whip you'd take some shortcuts too."

Empathy and a thirst for deeper understanding are the only safeguards to changing how you approach difficult situations with different people. It is our duty to empathize first and later strategize on how to minimize the conditions that others face daily. It does not make you a bad person if you are unable to do this, it simply makes your privilege your only lens to see life through. Something internally is so deeply entrenched that you either lack the ability to put yourself in others' shoes or that you are so far removed that you do not care; the only possible interpretations. Not many people are willing to humble themselves enough to not be judgmental in those moments. That is why liabilities exist for everyone in this world who has some sort of daily mountain to climb or obstacle to overcome. It is just time for society to move beyond their personal feelings and create what Martin Luther King Jr. coined as the "Beloved Community."

This lifelong experience brings us to the purpose of this chapter, which is to define what a rebel is. But in order to construct a new definition for what a rebel is we must deconstruct what we currently consider to be a rebel. Do me a favor: close your eyes and picture a rebel. Who or what do you see? In most cases, you envision a person who has consistently bucked the system and refused to adopt the customary practices of whatever environment you were in. If you were in school, it was that kid who refused to obey the classroom rules.

Maybe it is someone who is eclectic, smokes weed, and lives a life of a transient. Is it possible that this person is an artist of some kind with tattoos covering their body who has never adopted the corporate lifestyle? No matter what you see or where they are, I want you to discard this image. I cannot be clearer that this person is NOT a rebel. They are simply an individual who has chosen to live their lives by a different set of principles. We cannot judge them or treat them differently because they have made a choice contrary to one we have made. It does no one any good particularly not you.

They have already accepted the consequences, good and bad, for their actions and frankly could care less about your opinion of them. Do not waste your time thinking of those who do not value your opinion. Better still, get to the point where you do not level your opinion or your waste thoughts on people who do not have a place in your life. This is the definition of counterproductive thinking.

(RE)Defining Moment

Back to the topic at hand, we dive right in to define what a rebel is for the purposes of our journey together. Rebel (n): an individual who reflects on their cultural, historical, and social status which through that interpretation pursues autonomy from stereotypical outcomes. It was my intention to make sure that this definition was very clear and had a 21st century interpretation that was applicable.

A rebel is not someone who "bucks the system" but one who dedicates him/herself to never fitting into the actions of the masses. The only way to fully complete the transformation into becoming a rebel is to do as the great Stephen Covey said and "start with the end in mind." It is an imperative step that should be taken because most youth or young-at-heart are so accustomed with living solely in the moment. They fully subscribe to the YOLO (You Only Live Once) lifestyle, which does not place considerable emphasis in how your behaviors today can impact your tomorrows and beyond. So, the first step to becoming a rebel is having someplace to go and a dream or mission to accomplish.

My father never made college an option as we grew up but a

natural step after graduation from high school. He was very intentional about making sure that we made it and supported all his children every step along the way. Eli has no choice but to attend college and if he wants to attend somewhere other than Morehouse he must find a way to pay for it himself. Why is this the mandate? Because I am a firm believer when Proverbs says that "life and death are in the power of the tongue." This has been the reality for years and psychological studies substantiate this idea. Henry Ford said it like this, "If you think you can do a thing or you think you can't do a thing, you're right."

This is the reality that most of us have not come to grips with or been willing to accept that we take part in our own misery. We have the power to change our fortune whenever we decide that we want to believe something different and work to change it.

There is a mantra that I try my best to live by which is: Live today like I did nothing yesterday to contribute to my tomorrow. This means that I put it into my mind that I am operating on borrowed time and that I am not doing enough to make the necessary improvements that will aggressively move my life forward.

Some people would call this unhealthy or pessimistic thinking but I have succumbed to the process of hard work and preparation. I would much rather have the mindset of never being satisfied with what I produce rather than live a life wondering what if or worse why not me.

As I write these very words, I have already imagined myself being interviewed by Oprah and discussing how I came up with this concept. It can happen if I will myself to make sure that it does. Not saying that all your dreams will come true but I fell in love with the words of Norman Vincent Peale when he said, "Aim for the moon and if you miss you're still amongst the stars." So, it is only sensible to believe my wildest dreams wholeheartedly and then develop and apply a work ethic to make them attainable.

We have had earlier discussions about stereotypes and how they operate which is why it was important to discuss the idea of self-fulfilling prophecy. It can have miraculous effects on your life for the better or worse depending on the language that you use. For example, I refuse to say I am sorry to anyone but rather I apologize because I never want to begin to convince myself that I am anything less than brilliant or hardworking or innovative. A pastor of a church I regularly attended would conclude every service the same way by having the congregation repeat this: "the words out of my mouth will live in my future." Truer words never spoken yet there are people blind as to how this impacts their everyday lives.

The definition goes on to say that you should lead an autonomous life or one that requires an independent or freedom mindset. In our everyday lives, we become slaves to the professional demands and the logistical aspects that we are required to maintain. Even worse, our society has been intentionally designed to produce followers or people who try to "keep up with the Joneses." The principle issue with this is that if you are spending any considerable portion of your day watching others and mimicking their behaviors, style, lingo, etc. then you cannot spend that time finding your truest self.

There is a reason that the most charismatic characters in

history are those who fought against the current and against what was the most convenient. I love the way that Beetles front man John Lennon captured this idea saying, "I'm not going to change how I look or the way I feel to conform to anything... I'm one of those people." To be a rebel it requires this deep belief in self, what you are purposed to accomplish, and what you must offer the world. It is at times a lonely road and you will often turn around and find that you are standing by yourself, but this is a good thing.

Next as part of the definition there comes the word "interpretation," which could be the most subjective word in the English language. This has everything to do with bias and the way we formulate our thoughts and beliefs. Regardless of who you are or what you have, we always have the responsibility to interpret whatever comes in our direction, as previously discussed. In this case and for this definition it should be made abundantly clear that the interpretation is entirely internal. It is about finding a deeper understanding of who you are, where you come from and determining what that means personally and how it will make a difference in your life. So, everything I wrote about previously discussing the fact that I am a Black man and what that means is my truth. It is the most essential puzzle piece that I need to have the ability to think for myself.

I want to be extremely transparent about a few things in this moment. First, you do not owe anyone any kind of explanation about who, what, or why you exist. Unless they plan on doing some serious time in jail for your murder then they cannot do anything about who you are or what you believe. My personal belief is that

God made you flawless and no man can undo the masterpiece that he completed. Point blank. End of story. Hasta luego. So, one of the best things you can do to strengthen your resolve is stop being an apologist. One of my favorite lines from Drake is when he said, "Don't ask permission, ask forgiveness" because he encourages everyone to be unapologetically yourself. If you are constantly worried about offending others or concerned about whether you belong, then you will surely convince yourself that you do not. STOP IT NOW! I want you, the reader, to do something for me. Raise your right hand and pledge out loud this statement:

"I, _____, deserve the best life possible and I, _____, have the right to take it through hard work, persistence, and force if necessary.

I, _____, will not apologize EVER, EVER, EVER for simply being me but rather embrace the idea that I do not fit in at all times. May God help anyone who gets in my way because _____'s future is mine for the taking."

Now for everyone who stepped over this without saying it, go back! Read it aloud until you start believing the words yourself. Particularly as an outsider or rebel, there will be times when you must encourage yourself. "Sometimes you have to encourage yourself. Sometimes you have to speak victory during your test. And no matter how you feel, just speak a word and you will be healed. Speak over yourself," are the lyrics to one of the few songs that got me through my Morehouse years. Thank you, Donald Lawrence.

No one is free from bias. I thought I would reiterate that fact in this moment because it is essential to know that. One of the most revealing moments of my studies in history was the idea that history is 100% subjective. It was a hard pill to swallow that there was no such thing as objectivity because we all have the burden of bias that we carry. So even as we only report facts it is the manner in which we report those facts that holds the biases. There is no escape from it and everything that comes along with it EXCEPT to be aware of its existence.

As you reflect and review and rethink any situation or scenario you will become or should become more in tune with yourself. "Follow effective action with reflection. From the quiet reflection will come even more effective action," remarked Peter Drucker which captures the idea of how reflection plays a major role in the lives of rebels.

We can act strongly or boldly or aggressively aplenty but if you have made no consideration as to how it will impact your standing then you will move nowhere. The truth is that the world we live in does not care who you are until you first reflect someone who knows oneself.

Have you ever thought about the scrutiny that the rich and famous are under as they simply walk through everyday life? How would you handle popular society constantly imposing itself upon you? I do not know this from experience (yet) but I do know that the only way to keep a strong sense of self is to be able to judge your action or inaction for yourself. The much maligned and rightfully demonized comedian Bill Cosby once uttered these powerful words, "I don't know the key to success but the key to failure is trying to please everyone." Much like any deviant or person who breaks the mold, you must be willing to trust yourself and operate on the basis that you know best. By all means, I encourage you to seek wisdom from those who have walked the path that you are on; there is special value in that. Nonetheless, you must be able to see and appreciate the world through your eyes to make an impact.

With that being said, it is not always something that society will agree with or even support. The 19th and 20th century anarchist Emma Goldman wrote, "The most unpardonable sin in society is independence of thought." This simply highlights the fact that when you are different that you will be faced with people who want to change your thinking to fit everyone else. I contend that you should resist this at all costs. The world is filled with leaders who were talked out of their dreams, have aged, and become followers.

Self-reflection is the key to being able to deter the influence of these voices. But another reality is that you cannot shield yourself from the realities that society offers. One of my deepest held beliefs lives in the idea that, "Neither the life of an individual nor the history of a society can be understood without understanding both," which tells me that you should be in society but not of it. There is a mentality that is essential to progress, but that mentality is part and parcel to you having a firm understanding of self.

To conclude the definition, there is an insistence to dive into your cultural and historical background and determine what it is that you can decipher about yourself. For myself, I have the responsibility to study Black culture and history and through this knowledge I can better decipher who I am or have the potential to be. One of the most pressing issues with history is that it is too often told to not make anyone uncomfortable. The problem with this is that it requires a watered-down version of the truth. So, when considering everything that you learned in K-12 education about Black history, we have been relegated to Trans-Atlantic Slave Trade, Crispus Attucks, Civil War, Reconstruction, Harlem Renaissance, and the Civil Rights Movement (primarily MLK) in that order, all in one month.

If your foundational understanding of history began with enslaved ancestors, it would encourage someone to believe that the bottom is where they belong or what they deserve. The psychological impacts of such education are vast and pervading, yet it is our current model of educating young Black people on their culture. It is one of the most obvious benefits of privilege identified in our education system, because it means that history, which again is not objective, is fashioned to create villains and heroes. This is the reason that a deeper understanding of your own culture is so imperative to dispelling any biases that are created by others and self-maintained subconsciously. Civil rights activist and advocate for worker's rights Cesar Chavez said, "Preservation of one's own culture does not require contempt or disrespect of other cultures." So, your desire or natural inclination to discover more about and celebrate wholeheartedly the merits of your culture are well within your right. In fact, I would deem it an obligation to do so.

There is but one part of the definition that is left to explain the complete workings of what it means to be a rebel. Simply put, it is 100% about you, the individual, the person who is operating solo.

One of the hardest parts of being a rebel is the notion that you must strike out on your own and blaze a trail that no one else is travelling. At this point, I must reinforce the idea that being obstinate or defiant is not what makes you a rebel. It is the ability to define the world for yourself and make a conscious decision that you will live life differently. This too is an act of defiance, but the striving for progress is the defining characteristic that must be present.

Close your eyes and imagine yourself about to go on stage at the largest and most esteemed theater in your city. You have a speech to deliver and you have been preparing for months for this night. The time has finally come and you step out on the stage only to find out that no one else is in the entire building. That is what it will feel like to be a rebel. You are always going to be forced into a position that is uncomfortable and when you arrive you are going to realize that nobody is there to make you nervous or anxious or fearful but yourself. Being an individual requires an independent streak that will often leave you standing in a room of one. But more importantly...You must be OK with that.

If you are constantly looking for approval from outsiders and have a longing desire to seek fulfillment through other people, then you still have much to learn. No one will ever give you the approval or kudos or applause that you can provide for yourself.

No one has the right or power to determine how you feel about yourself unless you give it to them. There is something amazingly special about the ability to trust yourself more than the voice and opinions of those who are around you. Carl Jung, the famous psychotherapist, wrote," Resistance to the organized mass can be effected only by the man who is as well organized in his individuality as the mass itself." That suffices to say that you cannot be part of the crowd and stand out from it simultaneously. In the famous words of the late great Christopher Reeves AKA Superman, "Either you decide to stay in the shallow end or you go out in the ocean." The choice is always, is always, is always yours.

Need for Speed

Now that we have a firm foundation for why being a rebel is a necessity in today's world we can move on. Take note that you have heard it from scholar to entertainer to artist to dignitary, I hope that you can believe the notion that you are valuable.

This world does not change without people willing to force it to happen. It will require that you make some people uncomfortable and make some others unhappy and live a life that is contrary to others around you. Make sacrifices and adopt disciplines that others will not but in the end, it will be worth it. Why?

Because you will be your own man or woman and stand tall in the face of anything that may come your way. "If not now than when? If not, you then who?" This timeless rhetorical question that demands a response from the deepest parts of your humanity.

During my childhood and on my PlayStation console there

was a game called Need for Speed, which was a racing game of epic proportions. For hours and hours my brother, friends, and I would play this game and argue over who was the best. It was like there was some sort of prize that came from winning a race that never mattered and the results were never saved. The one thing that is to be gathered from this scenario is that even though it seemingly did not matter we still gave it meaning. We still played every game and every second of the game with a competitiveness to ensure that we were going to win this one game. Now in hindsight (which is always 20-20), I can see how miniscule or irrelevant these games were but you could not have told us that then; it was a matter of life and death.

I offer this reflection to connect the final characteristic of what is required to be a rebel which is a sense of urgency. With this key component on your side there is very little that cannot be accomplished. It is about a true recognition that time is never on your side and that no matter what you must make something happen now. One of the sayings I tell myself every morning now as part of ritual is that "I will work today like I did nothing yesterday to make my tomorrow better." The urgency in that statement is evident and very real because I understand that my son will keep growing and bills will keep coming and hunger will be back and dreams will go unfulfilled if I do not work as hard as humanly possible to progress in life.

I was told early in life that as a Black male in this world, "I have to work twice as hard to go half as far," a statement which I know now is the truth. There is not a damn thing in this world free and all I know to do and am equipped to do is get up every day with a chip on my shoulder. The one thing we all have the same amount of is time. Therefore, we must treat it as the most precious commodity we have. Not by only using it wisely but being able to push to attain more in that time. As a rebel, I should be diametrically different in the way I perceive my time and what goes in it. More importantly, I must be willing to push myself to limits that I, at one point, did not think were possible. This means that I should get comfortable being uncomfortable.

Once I get comfortable again, I challenge myself once more and push myself to the next level where I can become uncomfortable again. Nothing grows in comfort or when surrounded by convenience, which is why I refuse to believe you are supposed to swim with the current.

One of the most important things in the life of a rebel is not being a victim. A rebel is someone who reflects on where they are in life and makes the necessary steps to stir up change. We are all creatures of habit and one of the best things we can consistently do is make sure that those habits are moving our life in a direction that is positive. That personal discipline needed is the prerequisite to being able to offer solutions to the world's greatest challenges. There must be a desire to see your life move aggressively forward if you're going to be a rebel and influence the lives of those around you. No one can do this for you and no outside agitation can make this happen for you. I believe there comes a time in everyone's life where they must decide about who they are going to be for the rest of their life. I want to close this chapter sharing my story of what that catalyst was.

Heading into my junior year at Morehouse I went into it with a very succinct and what I thought to be; a full proof plan. I knew in that year I was going to serve on several executive boards for student organizations, start Morehouse Education Association to increase Black male presence in education, continue to live off-campus but in a better apartment, potentially cross into a Greek fraternity, and the list goes on. It was going to be a year of epic proportions and I knew how the script would unfold.

The one thing I did not account for was my financial aid not coming through and essentially having no money during the first semester of school. Luckily, Ms. Redd had moved to the Housing department from Student Services and was able to hook me up with a room. She is and always will be my guardian angel for this because I would have been homeless had it not been for her. Fortunately, I had a few dollars saved to be able to help with expenses for my son and to be able to survive 400 miles away from home. It was a blessing that I was able to secure a scholarship from Coca-Cola that allowed me to stay in school for the semester. Without these fortunate events occurring, I would have had to leave Morehouse that semester and statistically the chances of me returning would have been slim to none.

On the contrary, I was by far in the worse economic situation I had ever been in because those savings quickly evaporated. I could only afford to drive my car every couple of days (if that) because $20 of gas usually had to last me the entire month.

Every effort I made in the financial aid office came with

another hurdle to jump. During this one semester I probably spent 25-30 hours in their office; most people thought I was a work-study student. On top of that because I had set myself up to be so active on campus and with academics, 20 credit hours, I was virtually unable to work off-campus. Throughout college I always had odd jobs and was signed up with several temp services to be able to pull in some extra cash. It was a point where I borrowed money from everyone I could to send it back home or make sure that I could even eat some nights. I had in my possession only one suit (which is almost a sin at Morehouse) with pants that had a serious grease stain that I could not afford to take to the dry cleaners and two pairs of jeans both with frayed bottoms. Every pair of shoes I owned had holes in them and I would pray that it would not rain so my feet would be dry. I wore the same rotation of clothes and in November when the weather changed, I could not afford a coat so I wore the same Ohio State hoodie nearly every day. (Most people assumed this was because I had so much Ohio pride which I do but it was not the reason I wore it.) Once a social butterfly, I refused to take part in activities because of how poorly dressed I was or the fact that I simply could not afford to go out. Sounds like a sad story, right? Absolutely correct but the defining moment in this situation was when I decided to suffer in silence.

None of my family members or friends knew the extent to which I was struggling because frankly they would have done everything in their power to help. That is the opposite of what I wanted. I used these dire circumstances to force myself to dig deep and give myself the opportunity to lift myself.

There was any number of things I could have done to make my life easier or more convenient but remember when I said nothing grows in comfort? Well, I believed that then and now. I figured if I was to be bailed out of this situation then I would feel entitled to a bailout in the future for another situation and another. I made the conscious decision to fight for my progress and define in that moment who I was going to be. It taught me that I have another gear and a reservoir of willpower that I can tap into when necessary that will not yield until the desired outcome is reached.

It is so unbelievable critical for you to have this moment and be dependent on only yourself. It is such an essential part of your future growth that I need you to pause in this moment and consider a time where you have ever had to show amazing courage or resolve or persistence. It is not enough to always come out on top but you must be able to deal with adversity and prove your resilience.

Resilience is one of the most essential components to being able to handle whatever comes your way. So, I want you to think of that time and hold onto it as you continue to read more into this text. If by chance you do not have a story yourself do not worry about it, you will have one of these stories soon enough. But for the purposes of the book, I invite you to find someone that you admire and research their background to find an example; you will.

This story does not have to be as painful as mine or as troubling but it does have to be one that should inspire something in you. It should be something that you deem extraordinary. It should be by someone who you have deep aspirations to be like or attain their level of success. Even more paramount is that you must believe that you have this kind of power internally. I am here to simply tell you that you do and that you have more strength than you can ever imagine if you find the keys to unlock it. I am here to share with you that to become a rebel you should first learn what it means to REBEL.

In the chapters to follow were going to dive into the crux of the theory of change. At no point do I want to suggest that this method or the thoughts I share are the end-all-be-all to living productively in our society. But I do believe that they will provide you with a conceptual advantage; a head start if you will. I do not know if I am going to tell you something that you have never heard before but I will surely give you a fresh perspective and challenge you to think differently.

The rest of this book is straightforward and very direct. One of the things I pride myself on is an ability to navigate through all the white noise and get down to brass tacks. I believe that anyone who buys into the system and really looks to renew their mind will have an opportunity to change their life. I would never say that this work will be easy or the world is simply going to move aside and allow you to operate without obstruction; that would be a lie. I am telling you that if you change your perspective then you afford yourself certain privileges.

Conscious of the Rebel

"In essence, if we want to direct our lives, we must take control of our consistent actions. It's not what we do once in a while that shapes our lives, but what we do consistently."

-*Tony Robbins*

Time and time again, I have thought about this journey called life and been confused or frustrated, because I was uncertain about one thing or another. If you are a believer in astrology, which I am not (though I can admit that at times it is scarily accurate), it could be said that I can attribute some of this indecisiveness to being a Libra. All jokes aside, we have all been saddled with the burden of trying to figure out what is the best decision and what we will do when *THE* moment comes.

Oftentimes, we do not handle the situation as perfectly as we want and sometimes we just handle it poorly. If we counted all the times when we had a situation or a conversation that did not go as planned, we would be counting for days if not months. Nonetheless, 12AM brings forth a new day and we must continue onward. Life moves on with or without the situation being handled with amazing finesse or the appropriate grace. (Insert shrugs here). I am not saying that you should not do your best to handle every situation as best as possible, I am just saying that tomorrow is always another day to improve upon what happened today.

Human beings are creatures of habit, lovers of convenience, and aspirants for efficiency. We are these things simultaneously and there is constant conflict between them. At times, our habits may not align with what is most efficient. On other occasions, what we deem as convenient may lead to poor habits and negatively impact our effectiveness. So, there is this balancing act that we are all forced to perform every day of our lives. This, in part, leads to the poor handling of challenging situations that life throws our way. Yet, how we manage these very contentious areas of our lives will determine the progress we realize. These outcomes can be the difference between a prosperous life and one filled with turmoil. It essentially is the personal policy we use to dictate our daily behaviour. It is a critical component to how we determine the best route, one decision at a time, for us to take.

A long, long time ago I remember being down in Phenix City, Alabama with my girlfriend at the time, Elijah's mother, for her great-grandmother's 80th birthday celebration, way out in the boondocks of Alabama, a mile from the Georgia state line. It was during this occasion that all her great-grandmother's children came together to celebrate their mother. One had been ill for quite some time after being diagnosed with lupus. The afternoon following the celebration, the matriarch of the family called us to gather around the bedside of her ill child for prayer.

Several minutes later, I remember us all being on the porch and one of her sisters was crying about her pain and suffering. Big Ma, as she was affectionately called, told her daughter to stop crying because it was not going to do any good. Then she uttered words that I will never forget, "If you pray don't worry and if you worry don't pray. God's going to have His way no matter what."

These very words are what I carried with me through every trial and struggle that I have faced in my life since. It became abundantly clear that there were certain things that would always be outside of my control. With these things, and these things specifically, I had to learn to remove worry, doubt, and fear from the situation. Now I do not suspect that everyone is a believer in a higher power, but there is some added benefit to not feeling alone in the midst of struggle. I will concede that it is not the path that everyone is going to take. Nonetheless, there still must be some type of skill development around handling problems. This skill set is something that deals exclusively with controlling what you can. Knowing exactly what you have dominion over and exercising it as it is your birthright.

Consciousness is something that everyone has but not everyone commits themselves to use. Not everyone pays attention to the world around them and how everything impacts their lives. There are plenty of people who have made the decision to remain ignorant to what happens in their environment. I am not condemning this way of living but I do not endorse it.

I believe that it strips people of their God-given ability to self-determination. It makes people aimless and unfocused because they do not fully control their thought life. Thinking leads to action and action to growth, thus without consciousness of what is happening you can never control your circumstances. I cannot live with that as my reality and I would hope that you could not either.

There is a new craze in the world of youth empowerment, which is mindfulness. Mindfulness is just a fancy way of saying that a person is self-aware. That they consider everything that happens in their life and think their way out of every situation. They own each moment for what it is and challenge their personal status quo. Everyone does not have the natural ability to be able to do this nor should they be able to. There is always something that happens in life that demands that you become more cerebral, more thoughtful...more self-aware.

At the root of it all, being self-aware is little more than exerting control over your thought life. It helps you control your speech and manage your expectations of self and others. It opens the floodgates to your ability to place a premium on who, what, and why things deserve your attention.

After my mother left, I had massive trust issues, particularly with women, that consumed my everyday life. I did not share much of anything with anyone and dealt with every issue by myself. It was a lonely experience, but it did something to change me for the better. Unlike most people who retreat to a shell, I was a highly active and social teenager. I had friends and family spread across the city and I was thrust into learning how to navigate unfamiliar spaces quickly. Even though I knew hundreds of kids from around the city, I never confided in any of them. We had positive and friendly relationships but it was never cause to let anyone know how I was truly feeling. I thought my way through every situation and was a very calculating kid, in and outside of school.

I have no problem acknowledging that I was no angel when I was in my teenage years. It is funny to think back on those years with all the vandalism, fighting, and other crazy stuff we engaged in. By nothing but the will of God and making up my mind to be different was I able to escape some of the perils that my peers faced. I cannot say that I was ever the smartest or most athletic, but I believe I could always decipher when an action was going to lead to a place with serious consequences. There was always this intuition I had about certain actions or when I would be very close to getting in trouble. I did not always adhere to this "sixth sense" but I was aware that my behaviour and my future were tied to my decision-making.

Just a few weeks ago, I came together with most of the guys who I grew up and did stupid things with. The scary thing about it was that I realized that I did mostly everything they did and many of them have faced jail time or some other consequence that altered their lives. As I sat in a room of 20 plus, I realized that I was one of two to graduate from a four-year institution. Yet, I was the only one who could move out of the state to go to school. It deeply saddened me that this was my truth when I have nothing but love for my brothers. We grew from young boys to men raising children together yet our paths were diametrically different. I attribute this to demanding elders, a decision, and a tragic event during my junior year of high school.

I was the authority at Princeton High on parties all around the city because of my network of people I knew growing up. Every weekend I would know about five to six house parties around the city and had to decide where I wanted to enjoy my time. After a while, I would have dozens of text messages each Friday and Saturday asking where they could find a place to kick it. The problem with these parties was that in Cincinnati we always fought. Fought because we did not know someone, because they were from another neighbourhood, or fought for the sake of ego. All of this fighting had begun to wear on my conscious because some people were seriously getting hurt or being arrested for these occurrences. So, I made a firm decision that I would no longer attend any parties because I was committed to escaping Cincinnati. I knew the only way I could do that was through college. This was the decision.

The tragic event took place on Christmas Eve when I was begged and prodded to go to this party at a club called Legacy that was having a teen night. I said I did not want to go but I was the one with a driver's license. After about an hour of begging, I finally conceded and drove to round everyone up. When we arrived the parking lot was packed and it seemed like this was *the* party to be at. As we were making it across the parking lot we see the doors swing open and hundreds of people pouring out. I stopped to ask someone I knew what was happening and of course a fight had broken out inside of the club. Within a matter of seconds, the fight started back up outside and chaos ensued. Not soon after there was gunfire and people scrambling everywhere.

Chanel Jordan was her name. She was a little bit older than I was, graduated from a rival high school, but her boyfriend was my brother's age and we all grew up together. She had a very young daughter and this was to be their second Christmas together. She was hit with a stray bullet in her head and died on the street bleeding out. To be honest, I am not sure if I physically saw her laying there or if I imagined the whole thing, but I know I still have the image in my head. I still see her big brown eyes and long beautiful head of hair gushing blood. I thought of her daughter waking up on Christmas morning without a mother. Nonetheless, that was the breaking point for me. That was the moment when I knew beyond a shadow of doubt that I had to escape. I could not be a part of what I used to be. I could not hang with all the people I used to hang with. I could not pretend that I was about a wild lifestyle anymore.

This mindset and this tragedy unequivocally altered the direction of my life although it put me in isolation. I was isolated from friends I had hung with for years. I was cut off from social gatherings, parties, and other popular places. I knew that I could never go back and that I would never be the same. All I could imagine at that point was escaping from Cincinnati. Escaping from Lincoln Heights, the most economically depraved municipality in the state of Ohio. Escaping from a stereotypical outcome. I knew that my success would be my salvation and that loneliness accompanied the road less travelled. I did not know specifically where I wanted to be, but I knew it was not where I was. So outside of academics, sports, and work nothing deserved my undivided attention. Nothing meant more to me than escape and I knew that I would never feel safe until I did. I knew that I had to execute my plan.

D: DESTINATION

Every living being on this planet has DNA, which are the building blocks of our genetic code. This genetic code is something that we all have and that we all live with. It is the foundation of your physical traits, natural abilities, and even explains why as a 24-year old young man I began losing my hair. Many people believe that this will also impact how smart you can become or other indicators of how successful you will become. For the purposes of any rebel, we must expand the definition of DNA to also incorporate socioeconomic status, the family in which you are born, the environment that you are reared, the trauma your parents could not shield you from, and any other aspect of your life that was beyond your immediate control. These factors are of equal importance to explain how you turned out to this point. Once upon a time, we called these factors nurture, but now it does not serve the conversation.

Destination has its roots in the Latin word *destinare*, which means "determine, appoint, choose, or make firm," according to Vocabulary.com. To make a determination about anything you must be definitive, to appoint or choose you must be decisive, and to be firm speaks to consistency. These synonyms make it clear that to have a destination is very much so a commitment to yourself. You make a personal vow to not be deterred or distracted or ever quit on yourself. I can still remember attending the graduation of the Class of 2009 from Morehouse and seeing the ceremony for the first time.

I thought my reaction would simply have been one of pride for that extraordinary group of young men, but it was so much more. I envisioned myself getting across that very stage, being celebrated by 10,000 people in that way, reaching the destination my dad required of me. With Dr. Mays looking on, I understood that day that perseverance was not optional but it was demanded.

My dad never told me how to get it done, but he made sure I was resilient enough to get the job done. "When you turn 18, you're either going to be working, you're going to go to college, or you get the hell out of my house," were the words my dad always told us growing up. Then he went on to say, "And you're not allowed to work without having a degree." I thank him daily for holding me to this standard.

One of my favorite scriptures, one that I read at the funeral of my adopted mother, is Ephesians 4:1-2: "Therefore, I, a servant for serving the Lord, beg you to live a life worthy of your calling for you have been called by God." It is incumbent upon any person to believe that success is not in the things that you accumulate, but in the destinations that you reach. We should be willing and able to process the journey we are placed on from the second that we are birthed.

I still remember the day my dad left New Student Orientation at Morehouse saying, "I'll be back at graduation. You know what to do," as if he knew, beyond a shadow of a doubt, that I was going to complete my mission. I will never forget that moment because my dad never set foot back in Atlanta until my graduation. It is my highest honor to have fulfilled the mission my dad set out for me. It was through his clarity that I benefited so greatly and allows me to be writing to you. Nonetheless, this was the end of the destination he set for me and where I had to then determine my next destination. I was so focused on the task at hand that I never acknowledged that there was a life after college to consider. I fell short, I made mistakes, I missed opportunities, but I grew from my ignorance. I knew that I had to change myself in order to change my circumstance. I knew I deserved to thrive.

There is something distinctly powerful about feeling in control over one's life. It is liberating and intoxicating, yet in most cases it is simply a relief. Because it is not something that everyone gets to attain, there is something to be said about the wave of peace that comes from self-determined stability. For people who come from very adverse circumstances, the possibility to reach this level is often so distant that it seems impossible. The problem with poverty is that it stifles exposure and cripples access. It changes the way that you see the world; it is glasses with unclean lens. It challenges your ability to be optimistic about the future and without ample exposure it shields you from seeing opportunity as it is intended.

Over the course of my life, I have never experienced extreme poverty outside of the struggle right after I graduated from college when I crashed on couches and often slept in my car. I would not genuinely appreciate the depths of poverty if I did not recognize that I was in the privileged position to have a car to sleep in or anyone willing to let me sleep on their couch. I must accept that the God has always seen fit to leave me something to leverage for our, Elijah and I's, survival. Yet, the funny thing about simply living to survive is that your situation does not allow you the luxury to determine the direction you wish to go. What happens in the process of survival is that your basic needs become the principle objects of your desire. Food, shelter, and clothing become the principal foci for the operation of your life. You hone in on the bottom of the pyramid of Maslow's hierarchy and do not have time to focus on much else. After a while you become completely desensitized to the fact that you have other needs that should be satisfied. I was there. I remember that aimless existence.

Janelle Monae, who I fondly remember buying *Metropolis* at Spelman's Market Friday, once remarked, "We don't all have to take the same coordinates to get to the same destination." I interpret this to mean that there are many ways to get to the same end goal, which is most definitely true. No one can ever state that there is one way to reach any goal; not even in this book. It is my earnest prayer that this book reaches multitudes of people, but part of the beauty of knowledge is that it has no owner. It lives as free as the one who garners it and wields it for his or her benefit. When we talk about reaching your destination we should first understand that it is to our benefit to have clarity of purpose. Brendon Burchard once proclaimed that, "clarity comes with simplicity."

Have you ever made detailed, structured, and well-thought out plans? Did they ever unfold without a hitch? Chances are that they did not. There are almost always speedbumps, twists, and sharp turns on the road to your destination. No matter what you try to plan there always should be room to adjust and recalculate.

Clarity has nothing to do with the small details but rather everything about how you will make efficient and proportionate steps toward your goal. These types of steps add context to the distance that you must travel. It brings everything into focus because it does not allow for your mind to wonder off. It has structure and a resoluteness about itself that is necessary to bring clarity to the overall vision. This leads us to the next step of the process of understanding how to determine success for yourself.

From senior year of high school on, I knew I was going into education. I wholeheartedly believed that it was my destiny to impact the future growth of dozens of youth. I wanted to change the lives of young people. I wanted to become one of the greatest educators to ever grace this planet. None of that has changed in the last decade. But when I started out I wanted to become a teacher, then a principal, then a superintendent, then the U.S. Secretary of Education. The goal never changed but I never confined my role in society to a finite job title. When I was exposed to more, my vision for my life grew exponentially. If I were a teacher at Princeton High, I could teach roughly 120 students per day. As U.S. Secretary of Education, I could write policies that impact 50 million students annually. Whether it is 120 students or 50 million, I want to be an amazing educator who impacts youth lives. The *destination* is the impact not the position; it is my purpose in life.

In the words of the late great Prince, "we are gathered here today to make it through this thing called life." We have all made it to this very moment due to a chain of events that lead us here. It was not a matter of chance but one of fate. Now there may be people who say that they do not believe in destiny because it supposes that there is a cosmic power at work and that they are in control. However, I would venture to say that most of these people are believers of cause and effect. I believe it behoves every person to believe that their every action or inaction will have some sort of impact on the direction of their lives. This belief is what will determine where you go in life. Either you choose the route that you take or it will be chosen despite you. We should get there but more importantly we must know how we will make that happen.

N: NAVIGATION

After attending two college tours visiting Historically Black Colleges and Universities (HBCUs) in my freshman and junior years, I knew that I wanted to spend my college years at one. My choices had narrowed to Howard University in Washington D.C., Hampton University in Virginia, or Morehouse College in Atlanta, GA. I would not even consider a university in Cincinnati unless I would be endowed with a full academic scholarship and then some. Hampton was a distant third and was the least appealing because I knew I wanted to be in a major city. Howard was in the epicenter of politics and I had loved the two times I had been in the District as a child. Plus, at that point, I aspired to become a lawyer. But Morehouse was in the Black Mecca, Atlanta, Georgia where I had spent countless Thanksgivings and summers down there with family. I knew so much about the city and loved so many people who resided there. I knew it got hot in the summer and that snow was almost considered an urban legend. The weather was literally all that gave it the edge over Howard. So, it was at the top of my list.

In my roles as a college advisor and career specialist working with Cincinnati Youth Collaborative, I can see that the reasoning for my choices was probably off-base. Reflecting on it, I could have likely been able to save some serious money by staying in the state of Ohio. Chances are I would have received a comparable academic education and would have been able to participate in much of the same work at half the price of an HBCU. None of that mattered to me though. I was dead set on attending a school that was dedicated to the education of African-Americans. Morehouse being all-male with all-female Spelman College next door was the icing on the cake for me.

I knew where I wanted to be. I knew how I was going to get there. I knew that I was going to make it there by August 2007. I knew it would change my life, simply by being in the center of Black male education. I knew I could learn from people who were going to hold me to a high standard, after all it is the alma mater of Dr. Martin King, Maynard Jackson, Samuel L. Jackson, Spike Lee, Rev. Otis Moss, and so many other people who shaped America as Black men.

I was accepted into Morehouse in November of my senior year, a few weeks after turning 18, and it changed everything about the way I approached my remaining time in Cincinnati. I knew that my destination was set and that my world, the Cincinnati that I had known, was not all the world was offering me. I knew that there was something more out there for me and that I had to be even more cautious if I was going to realize it. I vividly remember sacrificing my social life to a great extent to continually position myself. There were friends I had been with for years that I had to distance myself from. I do not condemn any behavior that does not harm another human being, but I knew, then and now, that I could not always be around certain things. Here is the reality: the company you surround yourself with will determine your future particularly in pivotal, life-transitioning moments. I could have smoked weed daily my senior year of high school, but I had not reached college yet. When you have yet to reach your goal, you must make the decision that your future destination trumps every current association. Conviction to accomplish goals always must beat out convenience.

"We are all here for a reason on a particular path, you do not need a curriculum to know that you are part of the math...That's why I expose my soul to the globe; the world I am trying to expose to these little boys and girls," proclaimed J. Ivy on Kanye West's Never Let Me Down. When we think about the destination that we are purposed to reach, we need to know that it is about much more than ourselves. I will be the first person to admit that I am not motivated for myself. If it was all for my own personal gain, then I would be happy and content with far less. I could easily imagine myself teaching for the next 35 years and retiring having changed the lives of tens of thousands of students that I would have encountered. I just want more impact than that. There is nothing wrong with teaching as your life's work because we need more people pouring into young people, but I know that it is not enough for me. I know that my path will be one that requires that I move at a faster pace, that I reach more youth and across the world.

Whatever you do in life has a set of requirements that you must account for. I served as a Career Specialist working with the largest youth support service provider in Cincinnati. In this role, I help students clarify their goals and help them execute the steps to attain their goals. And sometimes I have to be the one to tell a student what their actions have afforded them; often it is not nearly as much as they assume.

Some students have a work ethic that affords them a 2.0 GPA but they want to attend a college that requires a 3.5 GPA. In these cases, and I see far too many, the student has a destination in mind and possible a career field chosen, but they have not placed themselves able to attain it. Having a destination is only valuable when you have a plan to reach it.

Do you remember when MapQuest first landed on the scene in 2000? This was back in the AOL dial-up internet days that younger people probably will not remember, but it was amazing. It was brand new, disruptive technology that did not require an expensive GPS system for your vehicle. It was a wave that spread across the country and saved some significant time helping people stop from getting lost in route to their destination. It saved time and saved gas money, which we can all agree are substantial commodities in our world today. I reference MapQuest instead of Google Maps because I want you to understand the idea of guidance not at your fingertips, and how revolutionary it can be when applied properly. When it comes to deciding where you want to go and what you want to accomplish, you must be willing to seek guidance. You must understand the process that, at its foundation, requires work, time, and money. As an educator, I can never be arrested or do anything that will possibly impact my ability to work with youth. How could I possibly fulfil my purpose in life without working with children? "How Sway?" It would be totally impossible! I know that there are sacrifices that I must make and other opportunities to turn down to reach my purposed destination. I know that this journey will, without question, be worth it. And when, not if, I hit trouble along the journey, I know that I would have changed enough lives for the frustration that comes as an educator to be inconsequential.

Imagine a young woman who wants to be President of the United States and believes deeply in her heart that she will be yet never studies politics. Envision a high school phenom who has all the God-given talent in the world to make it to the Olympics, but does not have the grades to be eligible to run track for his or her school team. Consider a high school student who wants to be an astronaut but who struggles with and hates science classes.

This kind of disconnect between where you are trying to go and how you are going to arrive is mind-blowing, but it happens all the time. This is particularly true when we consider all that poverty strips from its sufferers. It leaves people with a warped sense of reality to believe that dreams can magically be realized. There is a popular meme that talks about the journey toward success that states, "You can't cheat the grind... It knows how much you've invested. It won't give you nothing you haven't worked for." Everyone has the right (and frankly an obligation) to dream big, but your work ethic must match what your destination requires.

Imagine you are a 911 operator receiving a frantic call from a person who sees someone in distress that needs emergency medical attention. You have a brief discussion with the confused caller and hear that someone is bleeding out. They are dying right in front of them. Now imagine they hang up the phone and never give the address to the operator to send help. How would you be able to help save that person? It is not likely that you could because as always time is of the essence. Now imagine that the person lying there bleeding profusely is your dreams. That changes the sense of urgency, huh? Everyone has dreams of where they want to go but there is always a point where you will need some help. When you need that help you should be clear about what you need help with. When you are a young Black male or any young person, you will come across people who are more than willing to help you on your journey. But they are only willing to help you when you know exactly where you are going.

I will never forget when I had the fortunate opportunity to meet Roland Martin, famed correspondent and political commentator, at Morehouse. We were convened for Table of Brotherhood, a series of conversations leading the dedication of MLK monument on the National Mall. I thought it would be an amazing opportunity to speak with some of the key players there. I had a proclivity for being the last person to talk with the keynote speaker, which was a form of stalking them around the room to leave an impression. I had done this countless times throughout my time in Atlanta and it always turned out well. At the time, I was barely afloat as an entrepreneur and constantly tweaking the business model. I remember catching Mr. Martin right before he left the chapel and when I finally got face to face with him, I froze up. I could not put a complete thought together to save my life. As I was stumbling through my pitch, he stopped me saying, "Son, you are all over the place and obviously you wanted to talk to me because you followed me for a long time. But your time and my time are not the same, I have much more to do than you do. So, you have to be prepared with your ask." Boom.

It was the first time I had ever not executed in the moment and frankly I was embarrassed. It opened my eyes to the reality that I had to be decisive if I wanted help. I had to articulate where I intended to go and how they could help me get there. Mr. Martin will likely never know how he impacted my life, but his firm kick in the ass made me realize that time was a commodity that I had not given the proper respect. It added a serious sense of urgency to the work I was doing and the way that I approached people whom I admired. But this conversation made me more focused on what it was that I had to do and the sense of urgency necessary to get it done. I had to move faster and with clarity about the steps necessary to reach my destination.

I: INTENSITY

I am an impatient driver. I have no problem admitting that, but I do not have road rage. I know you are probably thinking that is what everyone says, but truly I do not. Whenever I get stuck behind a slow driver, my first questions are, "Where are you going and why do you not want to get there quickly?" It does not bother me if it is someone elderly or someone with poor vision or just a nervous student driver, I feel that everyone should have urgency when they are serious about reaching their destination.

Everyone criticizes Atlanta traffic and drivers but I love the idea that everyone drives with a sense of purpose, with a rabid desire to get to their end. Having a sense of urgency is among the most important attributes when going after your goals. I believe that for the person who wants to get things done, they should be obsessed with their use of time.

In complete transparency, as I write these very words, I still struggle with procrastination; it is my longstanding vice. There is always this sense that time is boundless and a peculiar confidence that I will get the job done before the deadline. I always make the deadline, but I do not always give the work the necessary care that it requires. It is something that I always will have to work on because I am such a laid-back individual. All the time. Without compromise.

I concede that there is something wrong with this approach, but the older you get the harder it is to change this learned behavior. Once upon a time, I thought that it was something seriously wrong with me, however I found that it is the best way I operate. I have attributed some of this to my attention deficit disorder, but before I was diagnosed I used it as motivation.

I can still remember being in the fourth grade when we had science projects that we had to present at our annual science fair. I can remember not telling my dad about it and waking up at 4AM the morning of to complete it. I would create a science experiment in my head and then fabricated the numbers all while putting together a train wreck of a poster board. In hindsight, it was a hell of a feat for a fourth grader, though it was still indicative of the problem I had. This scenario reminds me of one of the most quoted passages in the Bible which comes from Ecclesiastes 3 and reads:

To everything there is a season, and a time to every purpose under the heaven: A time to be born, and a time to die; a time to plant, and a time to pluck up that which is planted; A time to kill, and a time to heal; a time to break down, and a time to build up...

It is full of contrasting emotions and life phases that we all must pass through. These are essential components to factor into what lies ahead in our lives. A blueprint so-to-speak. More importantly, it makes it abundantly clear that everything has a designated time. Everything has a shelf life. Everything has an expiration date. Time is and always will be undefeated.

One of the ways to tell whether there is something powerful or poignant about a word is to check the words that accompany it. That is exactly what we are going to do with the word *urgency.* Its synonyms are desperation, necessity, pressure, and seriousness. They all speak to the emotions that should complement having a sense of urgency. There is also a sense that failure is in the air. When I have this feeling, I work harder and I focus more intently. Why? Because I understand that I have a responsibility to myself or to others that requires the completion of the task. There will always be a viable excuse you can use to get out of honoring your responsibility, but excuses have never made anyone stronger. Ever.

"Excuses are tools of incompetence used to monuments of nothingness and bridges to nowhere," is a quote I have heard for years now. It is a quote that I have posted on my classroom walls and that I simply do not tolerate when it comes to dealing with my students. At one point, I had a bucket for my kids that read, "NO EXCUSES," and it was filled with candy for my students. Either they would receive the reward or explain to me why they could not complete the task assigned to them. Life does not care about the obstacles that you must face. Unfortunately, it does not account for poverty, hardship, any death experienced, or any other barrier to progress that someone might face.

So, I never offer too much slack to young people when it comes to fulfilling duties, because the world never does. Depending on who you ask, they will tell you that this is an "entitled" generation of young people. That every one of the us believes that we are owed something in life that we do not have to work for. I think that they are correct to a certain extent as I see this sometimes in my own son, but I cannot blame any of them. He, much like all young people, reflects what their parents have allowed.

In the next section, REMEMBER, I will offer a detailed account of how we got to this point in American history, particularly with Black males. I cannot in good faith discuss intensity without addressing what fuels it in my life. One of the realities that we are all, meaning Black males, are faced with is that we have odds to overcome that no other group (outside of maybe Latino males) must deal with in this country. We have a standard to reach that most people would crumble if they were under such pressure.

So, when we discuss *intensity* it takes on a different meaning for us. It means that that feeling that you have of restlessness and that you are always behind everyone else in the rat race is genuine. It is real, it is powerful, and it will never cease. Is it fair? No, it is not.

Does that matter? No, it does not. Why? Because it is the cards that have been dealt, therefore we must move with an urgency like no one else. Want to hear the good news? We are built to withstand whatever comes before us. Our challenge can never be greater than our ability to handle it; God says so. Not saying that there will not be a time when you must ask for assistance or drop to your knees in submission, but I can assure you this is to your benefit.

When I came back to Morehouse after having Elijah during finals week of my freshman year, I became depressed because I was away from him. I felt that I was cheating my duties as a father for the college life. All of this changed one afternoon while on the couch in my apartment, when it hit me that the only way that I could make my time away from Eli worthwhile is through my achievements. I had to do more on campus and leave a legacy while I was there. This was the single greatest moment of clarity that I have ever had. I was finally awoken and I finally had a sense of urgency. I knew my destination was to become an amazing educator, I knew I had to get off the couch and move, and I knew that I was on a deadline, May 15, 2011, my graduation day.

Ironically, the only thing that allowed me to numb the pain of not being with Elijah everyday was building a life he would inherit in the future. I have no regrets because of the way I utilized my time. Because of the growth I realized, for the extended family, and network that Elijah now has at his disposal; it was time well spent.

Minutes turn to hours, hours turn to days, days to weeks, weeks to months, months to years, and before we know it we have lost more time than we could ever account for. We cannot operate as if time has no bearing on our lives, because that is exactly how we track our growth. The principal question that we should ask ourselves when we are investing great quantities of time is: Was the time well spent on making me a better person? Everything does not have to be life-enriching but you should not go years without making serious plans on how to continue to develop yourself. Time, as the most precious commodity we have, cannot be so heavily discounted that you never factor its cost. In America, there is a dollar amount associated with everything that we do and all the things that we enjoy. When you go to work, you are paid by the hour and if you are on a salary or are an entrepreneur you can calculate what your hourly wage would be as well. The saying that "time is money" is absolutely accurate. We just do not always take the time to see it that way.

We all must conclude that we are not invincible and that our very lives have an expiration date. We do not know when that date is, but we do know without question that it is coming whether we like it or not. We should be sure that we are spending our time on things that are worthwhile and that move us forward.

I have not owned any game system, PlayStation console, XBOX or Wii, since I was a sophomore in high school. I gave it away to a friend for free, which was completely unheard of. I gave it up because I did not have the time to play it anyway. Then after I reached college, I knew that there was so much more I could accomplish without it. Not saying that there is anything wrong with owning a game system or anything else you do to pass the time, but you must make sure that it contributes to your personal growth.

Anything done without moderation will eventually cause for it to become more of an addiction, and addiction is a struggle to control. We should be aware of where our time, which is the pacemaker for our lives, is invested. We must be in control of it as much as we possibly can be. Intensity is equally linked to the organization and mastery of time as it is motivation or ambition. Working to accomplish this level of mastery is the essential ingredient when you are trying to develop a more intense, fulfilling lifestyle. It is something that will require constant maintenance, but it is very much so possible.

It Demands an Answer

The way I define mindset has more to do with the questions that govern your life and those that dictate your behavior. They should be simple enough to demand straightforward answers and broad enough to force you to think deeply...at least initially. This running conversation in your head must demand something from you. It must challenge the status quo of your life without wasting time focusing on anything but the mission that lies ahead of you. It must be goal-oriented and solution-based thinking for it to move you closer to becoming the person that you can be. Each of the sections were purposely designed to ask specific questions to progress your life. Destination asks, "Where am I going?" Navigation inquires, "How will I get there?" Intensity demands to know, "When do I want to arrive?" All of them put pressure on you to think about what your future entails.

I purposefully did not reveal these questions until this point because I wanted you to think for yourself what each meant to you personally. I hope that you thought of an ambitious goal, of sound direction, and of the attitude or sweat equity required of you. All of which are required for you to process whatever life throws your way. It is my hope that you have clarity about what it is that you can control and what you have no governance over. You always have the ability to control yourself (and little more than that) until you advance in life. If you cannot master your behavior, how can you ever expect to master any arena of life? The simplest way to do this is to take out the time to answer these three pressing questions in relation to your life and your goals.

Famed author and radio personality, Earl Nightingale, wrote that, "All we need is the plan, the road map, and the courage to press on to your destination." This is the foundation of what destination is. It supposes that you can think beyond your present condition and visualize your future. If you can do that then you develop a vision for your life. That no matter the circumstance and no matter the present obstacle in your life you can see yourself in a better place. Having a destination for where you want your life to go is the basis for having solace amid any storm. We all have had dark days but without a destination, without a light that you can recognize at the end of the tunnel, then those days become hopeless and you become helpless. Without hope for a better tomorrow, we will always interpret a troubling moment as all the future has to offer us. To live in a life of despair, which far too many people do, is a willingness to trade in your dreams and to strangle your own imagination. We cannot afford it. It is too steep a price to pay when you consider that struggle is never permanent unless you, yourself and no one else, allow it to be. Knowing your destination offers a launch pad to your wildest dreams and deepest desires. Your destination is what your very spirit becomes attached to. It is what your soul yearns for more than anything else.

You must know that your destination is worthless if you do not have a plan to reach that dream. James 2:17, in the New Living Version, proclaims emphatically that, "faith by itself is not enough. Unless it produces good deeds, it is dead and useless." Dreaming is wonderful, and in fact encouraged, but so is the work that reality demands of you to bring those dreams to fruition. A destination is pointless if you cannot execute on what it takes to arrive. There are times when you will not know everything but more often than not when you move in the direction of your goal, things will fall into place. It does not always happen that way, but when you dedicate your behavior to reaching your goals, your destination, then things will happen that you never thought possible. I know this to be true.

My life is a testimonial that this is possible, but none of it would have been remotely an option if I never acted. You must be willing to invest yourself fully to reaching where you want to go, what you want to accomplish, and what resources are needed to do so. You must make up your mind that you will not be deterred from what it is that you set out to do. I am here to tell you that no one can stop you and that no one ever will once they see the determination you demonstrate.

One of my closest mentors once gave me a quote that has always stuck with me saying, "What some people use as justification, others use as motivation." All that says is that the way you perceive a challenge is what makes the difference in how you behave in response to it. The long and short of it is that we cannot afford to be thrown off the course of what we wish to attain. We must move with aggression as we execute our plan to attain our goals. "Now I move with aggression, use my mind as a weapon, cause' chances are never given they tooken like interceptions," are powerful words from Meek Mill; listen to him. Nothing in the world will ever fall into your lap without some provocation. I am a firm believer that the world is designed for anyone to be successful if you have enough knowledge, grit, and determination. But to get anywhere in life, you must have the necessary intensity to make it happen. You must have the resolve to determine the outcome of any situation that you are in. You must dictate the speed you travel your path. You must be the commander-in-chief of your own destiny. It is all within your reach... if you want it bad enough.

REMEMBER

"Nurture great thoughts, for you will never go higher than your thoughts."

-Benjamin Disraeli

History is one of the most important things anyone of any culture or background has. It is a recognition of the works of those who have come before us. It calls us to appreciate all the sacrifices made by ancestors in order for us to get to the place that we are today. Within history every man or woman can find a reservoir of strength and resilience through the cultural experiences of the past.

There is always someone who you can draw inspiration from through the amazing works that they accomplished or all the lives that a person touched. And it should not be any surprise that people often draw more inspiration from those who have similar heritage or similar ethnic backgrounds. Surely, we can learn and be encouraged by people of all races, but there is something powerfully aspirational about connecting with someone who looks like you. Someone who has a shared experience who can empathize with your journey.

Some of the amazingly revealing and often forgotten words of Dr. Martin Luther King were that, "We are not the makers of history. We are made by history." This giant of a man was a believer that he was but an actor in the struggle for Black humanity. That history had unfolded in a way that made it possible for him to serve in the capacity that he did. This is a belief that we, the human race, all should come to grips with.

No one is a tree without roots in this country, no one is

exempt from the past on which they stand. When considering the history of our country, these United States of America, we are so deeply conflicted with the struggle for racial unity, equality, and our inescapable interdependence. You cannot discuss America, with all its glorious history, without acknowledging its dark, shadowy past. It would be like sports without ESPN or schools' absent textbooks or Christianity subtracting Christ. They are inseparable no matter how much we continue to segregate it from the national narrative.

The history of America is profoundly grounded in racial identity, its relations, and the privileges and liabilities that it has afforded people of different races. This school of thought has been the predominant method that our society has been governed dating back to nearly two hundred years before this country's founding. It should not be a great surprise to anyone how entrenched that our thoughts and perceptions on race have transferred throughout history. Thus officially, we will breakdown what constitutes a bias. Bias (n): unique thought influenced and encouraged by unconscious interaction with another being; growth of such thoughts are unintentional and natural. Keep this in mind as we face some challenging truths in this chapter.

Much of the reason for this is policy, but much more comes from the crossroads where truth met closed minds. Sides have hunkered down and the battlefield between the two sides is filled with landmines at every step. It is the culmination of our collective and separate historical experiences that makes this divide so wide, so extensive that no one seems to be able to broach the touchy subject of race.

We must be clear about something before we dive head first into this chapter aptly named *REMEMBER*. No matter what I write in this chapter there will be someone who will call me a "racist." There will be another who will infer that I am a "race-baiter." One more will say "that I have to let slavery go and move on." Then maybe one other will reference writing like this as "ill-informed" or "reverse racism" at work. To all the above, I offer one simple rebuke in the form of a bar from hip-hop artist and friend Naj Murph: "You disagree? I expect that you should/ But small minds don't swim in deep thought or acknowledge they could." That is a dope way to say that regardless if we disagree there must be space for the potential for understanding. Truth always explains itself.

No one has the right to determine the depth or the breadth of pain felt by anyone else because you have not lived their experience. Everyone is uniquely positioned to live their own life and develop their own lens for which to see the world. Nonetheless, there are intersections where different individuals have a shared experience that informs their perspective. These crossroads can come in the form of race, gender, sexual orientation, socioeconomic status, or any other classification you can imagine. These are avenues that can lead to even more division or trails that can unite a people who, in most cases, have limited commonality.

Unfortunately, in today's society, chaos and controversy are the foundation of what passes for media coverage. Hell, it is often the key determinant on if something even makes the news. Thus, outside of trivial or inconsequential examples, there are very few celebrated, organic moments in our society that receive widespread attention. For example, how often can you say you see positivity on your local news in urban or impoverished communities versus the occurrences that you hear something negative? The disparities are astronomical because it is urban subculture that has been mystified, amplified, and demonized in our society, therefore always getting more attention. It could lead one to believe everything that they see about any group of people. It could even, over time, make someone wonder if the people who are consistently vilified could ever be as human as the rest of us? All things considered, I feel that America has found itself in a dark place when it comes to the demeaning rhetoric and unconscionable treatment of Black males. And as this is my experience, the only lens I have to dissect, it is where we must start.

In the recovery of the Great Depression, there were many policies that were created to get the country back on track. Famed humorist Will Rogers diagnosed the process as, "Money was all appropriated for the top in hopes that it would trickle down to the needy." This is how the term *trickledown economics* was born. It has been a long-standing theory that says that if there are more incentives for the wealthy then eventually it will reach the lower classes of our society. This idea ironically supports the common adage, "the rich get richer and the poor get poorer," because income and wealth disparities in our country are as high as they have been since 1928, the year before the Depression.

I reference this scenario for a very important reason, which is to say that when you want to have an honest discussion about the history of America it can never come from the top. One of the most commonly used African proverbs states, "Until the lions have their own historians, the history of the hunt will always glorify the hunter." It brings clarity, in my mind, that the history and narrative has always been told through the lens of majority society. It is heavily one-sided and I, as a Black male, have not been portrayed favorably. So, I want to take the time here, as we discuss history, to dissect what it is to be Black, male, and born in the USA. Advice: *Get comfortable being uncomfortable.*

No. 9 Should Have Been No. 1

I cannot remember the last time that I did not see a report on the news that another Black male was killed by an officer. The list of names has grown to an absurd tally from young men (and women) nationwide. What is worse is that there never seems to be justice rendered or equitable application of the law. Though I understand the problematic circumstances that exist in predominantly Black communities around the country, which include plenty of senseless violence, I still cannot comprehend policing in America. Countless reports have been released over the years to refute the notions that there is more crime in urban areas or that Black people abuse drugs more than their white counterparts. Nor that there is any distinctive difference between suburban and urban youth regarding petty crime. Regardless of all of this, the relationship between authority in America and Black youth has always been strained.

The confidence in the criminal justice system continues to be aggressively eroded whenever there is failure to indict or convict the killer of another innocent Black male. Whether it be when Zimmerman was acquitted or when Ray Tensing received a mistrial after killing an unarmed father in Cincinnati or when Cleveland's District Attorney failed to indict the officers who killed 12-year-old Tamir Rice, we have far too many reasons to be skeptical.

One might say that it does not make sense to be distrustful of the police and that they exist to protect and serve the "public good." I believe this is the idealistic essence of the police department, but that has not been the experience for those not afforded that privilege. This brings us to the crux of the matter, where the heart of the issue lies, which is the assumptions that persist in the execution of their police duties. It is much more than a bad egg or an isolated incident that happens, because it fits all the necessary criteria for it to be considered a systemic ideology. A serious and deeply complex pattern of death, destruction, and multi-faceted dismantling of communities of color through over-policing, disproportionate arrests, and mass incarceration.

One of the top films of 2015 was Straight Outta Compton, which depicted the rise and break-up of the ever-controversial hip-hop group N.W.A., who were said to have spawned the genre of "gangsta rap." They were among the most highly-combative figures to ever touch the music scene because what some would consider to be angry or aggressive lyrics toward police. Their most famous song is called "Fuck the Police," which was an indictment of the Los Angeles Police Department and the group's first-hand experiences of racially-motivated discrimination aimed at them. The most powerful line of the song comes from the first verse by Ice Cube when he says, "A young nigga got it bad cause I'm brown/ And not the other color so police think/ They have the authority to kill a minority."

The sad thing about this statement is that it was the truth decades before the 1988 song release and has been the truth nationwide since. In fact, the 1965 Watts riots were ignited by persistent police brutality as were the 1992 L.A. Riots that came on the heels of the acquittal of the police who mercilessly and unnecessarily beat Rodney King. There is a historical precedent that exists when it comes to our, the Black community, healthy distrust of the criminal justice system.

So, when in the 2001 riots rocked Over-the-Rhine, the community in Cincinnati our church resided in, when unarmed Timothy Thomas was gunned down by an off-duty officer it is a continuation of this history. And too when the streets restlessly protested in Baltimore due to the death of Freddie Gray or Ferguson with the death of Michael Brown or acquittal of his killer or Chicago with the unwarranted execution of Laquan McDonald, you must know that our pain is real and has been persistent.

The extrajudicial beatings, killings, and oppression of young people of color over the years has been part of a long narrative in this country that is just now being called to atonement by minority society. At the root of all the systemic mistreatment by authorities is an underlying fear that clouds the vision of those who are sworn to protect and serve. The consistent, troubling narrative about Black males found its way into the subconscious minds of those who, if unchecked, had Constitutional authorization to end or severely disrupt a person's life.

This narrative is that our society had to be protected from Black males. Black males are rarely seen as victims or in need of protecting but rather should be protected from. No matter the color, age, or any other characteristics of a Black male, we strike fear in the hearts of our society simply because of our presence. Yet this should be expected. Therefore, the rule-of-thumb is "that if you ain't getting [arrested] stay the fuck from police."

We, Black males, have been labeled for nearly half of a millennium as ignorant, violent, uneducated, emotionally unstable, and uncooperative savages. Now there are plenty of people who have defied these stereotypes, but there is not a Black male in America who does not have to answer to them. We have been fitted with these labels, had it fire-branded on our skin, had it stained on our very existence, and they can never be removed. Should we feel ashamed of who we are? Society would say so yet we have the uniquely unenviable position of not being able to afford it. We must numb ourselves and close our ears.

There is no time for shame or discontent when your entire being, your very essence, the depths of your soul are fixated on survival. As a youth, you must maintain focus on surviving to be able to live long enough for your dreams to be born into mere infancy. After you have succeeded in surviving then (and only then) can you graduate to thriving. At that point, far later in life than most of our white male counterparts, and only at that point, do you move into building a sustainable future for yourself, spouse, and children you are responsible for. And after all that surviving, all that dreaming, all that blossoming, and all that building, it only requires one officer with unchecked biases and an itchy trigger finger to take my life or worst...my son's life.

Debt Paid in Blood

I remember the tears flowing from my eyes when the verdict was read exonerating the killer of Trayvon Martin. Outside of the fact that there was a demonization of a dead Black boy who was without question the victim in that case, it was a realization that I must raise my son in a place that does not value his life. It was a wake-up call for me that I do not have the good fortune to raise my son the same as other parents in majority society.

There are certain things that must be accounted for that will always factor into his upbringing that will increase his chance of survival. For example, I have not bought Elijah a toy gun of any type or color or size because of what happened with Tamir Rice and the fact that Black boys are rarely (if ever) given the benefit of the doubt when it comes to law enforcement. There are so many factors that play into what makes up the bias of law enforcement that exists when it comes to Black males. All of which must be accounted for in my parenting.

One of the biggest stories during the 2014-2015 NFL season was the suspension of Adrian Peterson for the discipline of his four-year old son, and the subsequent images that were released from the incident. It showed the scars on the legs and behind of the boy after he got in trouble for disobeying the rules of his father. One of the most troubling and revealing aspects of the entire experience was the discourse that followed in the reporting of the incident. The Black community completely understood what the boy had endured and the state of mind that AP was in. Majority society was not as understanding and was absolutely shocked that any child receives a whooping with a switch, a small tree branch, in that manner. Though I do believe that AP went a bit too far, which he admitted at his son's doctor appointment far before it ever hit the press, I believe that it made sense. As someone who was abused, I do not believe that you should ever use a weapon of any kind on a child. I am a firm believer that you use your hand or nothing. Period.

Nonetheless, nothing troubled me more than when AP missed his moment to be clear as to why it was necessary. AP did not share the most essential part of why we, the Black community, never spare the rod with our children. In our world, in Black America, in our American society, we cannot afford timeouts or slaps on the wrist. Why you may ask? Because the world does not offer those to Black males. There are always harsher consequences and a paucity of leniency for Black males from school discipline to law enforcement to judicial courts, which lead to inequitable suspensions and jail sentences. That is why I have no problem sharing with Elijah that the rules are different for him as a Black boy rather than his white classmates.

It was Bill Gates who said that, "exposure from a young age to the realities of the world is a super-big thing." That is why when female family members and friends chastise me for being too hard on Eli, I explain that I do it now so that police do not have to do it later. Frankly, I trust my parenting over their policing any day, and there is not a Black parent I know that would not agree. Black males all play a part in a high-stakes poker game where our opponent has all the face cards. We must play the game as close to perfect and it still may not be enough to win. So, I cannot afford, as a parent, for Elijah to believe that he is like everyone else when society tells him differently.

"What's the price for a Black man's life? / I check the toe tag, not one zero in sight/ I turn on the TV, not one hero in sight/ Unless he dribbles or fiddles with mics," comes from a verse from J. Cole's January 28th off his Forest Hills Drive album. This one line summarizes the situation that Black men are put in on a regular basis. Not only does it highlight all the sentiments about raising our children differently, it also addresses the persistent images that are perpetuated about Black men.
Highlighting the fact that Black males are too often only associated with sports and musical prowess and not academic or any other form of success.

It was mentioned before that 7 in 10 images of Black males on local news programming refer to some negativity. For this reason, I cannot expect anything outside of the stereotypical perceptions when interacting with Black males. It would be foolish to expect that society (and the individuals in it regardless of race) would not be influenced, to a great degree, by this. Couple that with the constant violence that permeates due to how drugs penetrated our communities particularly during the crack epidemic, and we have a powder keg. This combination as well as the vilification of crack, but not cocaine, set the stage for a wild west of stereotypical imagery of Black males for years to come.

It was not that cocaine and later crack was used any less in more affluent areas, but it was all about the demonization of who was using it. It directly relates to what perceptions have been developed over time and how they play out by those in authority. Drugs have always been something that has been prevalent in our society, but it was not until there was widespread violence that it became more of an issue. This is that all-important moment to address the systemic issues that have compounded drug trade and use in minority communities.

After reading the series of Huffington Post articles by my dear friend Renaldo Pearson, I was greatly moved by the depiction of America's judicial failings as, "The Sleeping Giant of Mass Incarceration." The funny thing about giants is that they are always visible, and those who witness them are always in constant state of amazement in the size of them; stay with me. So, when we have a culture of mass incarceration that was spurred by the "War on Drugs," we have a giant problem that forever changes the narrative surrounding drugs in minority communities.

In Pearson's Open Letter to Nelson Mandela before his passing about mass incarceration, there were some stark figures that had to be accounted for and contribute to the epidemic. He wrote this in his article:

> *"...One-third of adult black men have been labeled as felons for life, primarily through the now-glaringly unjust 'War on Drugs.' Indeed, in less than 30 years (since 1980),*

the penal population went from 300,000 to more than 2
million, with drug convictions accounting for the majority
of the increase (two-thirds of the rise in the federal
inmate population and more than half of the rise in state
prisoners."

When you incorporate the call from the highest office in the world, President of the United States, for roughly twenty years things got more intense. It started with Nixon when he declared drug abuse to be "public enemy number one" in 1971, and put it on the minds of all Americans. Special thanks must go to the 1981 TIME Magazine cover, *Paradise Lost? South Florida*, which brought the cocaine trade to coffee tables nationwide and demonized Cubans and Colombians in the drug trade. Next, we had the "Just Say No" campaign by Nancy Reagan and President Ronald Reagan who passed the Comprehensive Crime Control Act of 1984. The Sentencing Reform Act established mandatory sentencing guidelines for particular drug crimes including 100-to-1 crack to cocaine possession ratio, as well as a later amendment that introduced the "three strikes" and a life sentence. Many prefer to glaze over the fact that C.I.A. and U.S. Marine Corps was linked to the flow of drugs into the country from Costa Rica; I will never forget. Fast forward to the next administration when the "War on Drugs" was spearheaded by President George H.W. Bush to quall the flow of cocaine into the U.S. Lastly, we must pay homage to President Bill Clinton for his Violent Crime Control and Law Enforcement Act, which lead to 100,000 more officers for community oriented policing, $9.7 billion of that went to construct new prisons, eliminated funding for inmate education, and the expansion of death penalty offenses to include drug trafficking.

None of this registers into the conversation about self-sufficiency and the ability to be able to be successful in this world. Consider if one-third of Caucasian males or roughly 33 million people were holders of felonies and what the economic impact would be on their communities. Now wrap your head around the words of Furious Styles from the '90s film classic *Boyz n the Hood* when he said, "We don't own any planes, we don't own no ships. Now we are not the people flying and floating the [crack] rock in here." It was an indictment of system that had been bolstered through government support, yet exposed and neglected in the mid-80s.

Now use your imagination to ponder this existence described by Dr. Michelle Alexander, who wrote in *The New Jim Crow: Mass Incarceration in the Age of Colorblindness,* "[Felons] can be denied the right to vote, automatically excluded from juries, and legally-discriminated against in employment, housing, access to education, and public benefits, much as their grandparents and great-grandparents were during the Jim Crow era." So, when you hear a politician or news anchor claim that there should be less crime and more men in minority communities as fathers, challenge them. You should now have a better understanding that this was a byproduct of design not some innate proclivity to engage in criminal activity. If you believe so, you are openly displaying your bias. Check it.

Once you introduce 100,000 new officers into poorer

communities who have been conditioned then trained to strengthen the War on Drugs through Broken Windows policing then you have a recipe for systemic disaster. Based on who was demonized heavily in the years leading to '94, we filled inner cities with people who were encouraged to profile, and in some places, *stop and frisk* citizens in urban communities.

This obviously would lead to higher arrest rates in less affluent areas and the consequences were of course legal and permanent. Add the privatization of prisons coupled with the Thirteenth Amendment's clear language that involuntary servitude is illegal "except as a punishment for a crime whereof the party shall have been duly convicted," and we have the birth of the Prison Industrial Complex. "[Dr. Martin L. King] said, 'law and order exist for the purpose of establishing justice and that when they fail in this purpose they become the dangerously structured dams that block the flow of social progress," as it was cited by Pearson's article. Even President Bill Clinton himself said that his policies regarding mass incarceration were significantly flawed. The consideration of social progress is a much more difficult thing to imagine when you have these liabilities to consider when you are a man of color.

With all of this as the backdrop to the War on Drugs, it created an atmosphere that was very contentious towards men of color. Given the fact that this war has been covered on the news nightly for 30+ years, can you truly blame majority America for associating drugs with people of color? Not at all, but that is exactly why I am writing to you.

When Fox News Anchor Bill O'Reilly can equate Dr. Marc

Lamont Hill, simply for being a Black man, with looking like a drug dealer while he was a Columbia University professor, we have a serious problem; and this was in 2010. So, when I tell you that there is persistent impact on the minds of the masses still today, you can believe me. Furthermore, when you consider that nearly every drug dealer depicted on TV and in film is a person of color (barring the meth-focused, Netflix binge-worthy show Breaking Bad). It is much like many of the villains in 70s and 80s films were Russians; pure propaganda. I am no conspiracy theorist but I do believe that there has been a clear pattern established and subsequently a societal bias developed.

The Cost of Admission

This bias or leaning to equate crime with a skin color has been one that has pervaded in America since the dawn of our forced relocation to this country. Even when you consider the foundational reasons behind why Africans were stolen from the shores of West Africa, we must look at how skin color played a significant factor. In our agrarian society of the 16-19th centuries, indentured servitude among other people of European descent was not economically advantageous enough. There was also this little problem of having to acknowledge their humanity. Secondly, Native Americans were struck heavily by disease through the distribution of small pox blankets as well as a hail of bullets by earlier settlers. Not to mention, that they were on their own lands, so when the going got tough many of them would disappear without a trace. So, the economic geniuses of our country, in concert with most Western-

European nations, turned their focus to Africa. Why Africans? Advanced knowledge of how to build a thriving agrarian trade, no knowledge of the landscape in the Americas, and the most important fact that it could all be justified based on race.

Outside of the obvious which was that Africans in the Americas would be easily identifiable, slavery has deeply-bigoted roots and justifications that made the slave trade permissible. These roots grew from The Bible and with a corrupt interpretation of Genesis 9:25-27 about government forums i.e. Parliament and the desire to keep an edge over rival commercial nations. It would be disingenuous to try to paint a portrait that slavery did not exist in Africa prior to the Trans-Atlantic Slave Trade because it did. The key difference was the manner in which it was carried out. No slave trade in the history of the world was ever more gruesome and morally bankrupt than that of the British and its colonies in the Americas. Estimates range upwards to 100 million Africans were killed on one of three stages en route to becoming slave laborers: 1) during the melee in remote villages to capture men, women, and children, 2) during death marches from their village to the African coast to a slave port, or 3) while aboard a slave ship crossing the Atlantic Ocean. And to be clear, little to nothing is known of these deaths as few were ever documented. It makes you wonder how many African corpses line the ocean floor in the Atlantic? Death has always been a major part of the narrative of people of African descent in America.

The social sciences were always something that captured my attention and when in high school, I took every class possible that I could. Nothing captured my attention like history, which is why I later decided to major in it when I got to Morehouse. One of my favorite professors in the department was Dr. Larry Spruill, who wrote the definitive dissertation about how media, particularly photography, changed the narrative during the Civil Rights Movement. One of the major images that Dr. Spruill discussed with us was that of Emmett Till, the young Chicago boy who was lynched in Money, Mississippi for whistling at a white woman. He dove into how Mamie Till, his mother, defiantly held an open casket funeral for her slain son and how that image circulated through the nation. In 1955, lynching never had a face, though it was widely known that it was a common practice since the Christmas Eve of 1865 founding of the Ku Klux Klan. Over the next 100 years, there were nearly 4,000 documented, keyword: documented, racially motivated lynchings in America. Keep in mind that this does not include what was considered legal force used by police or others with so-called authority. This was the era of Jim Crow, an era of *de jure* segregation, that made it impossible for there to be a level playing field for Black people in this country.

At this point of the chapter, I wonder if you are in anyway uncomfortable? I certainly hope so. No one should be able to hear the truth about the Black experience in this country without it making them question our society. It turns out that we, America, are among the most hypocritical nations to ever maintain power. When you consider that the Declaration of Independence claiming "life, liberty, and the pursuit of happiness" was written by a slave owner. When you reference that America created a Bill of Rights that was to be applied to all Americans, while the gross domestic product of our budding nation was dependent of the inhumane treatment of an entire race of people. Then when you do your research and find that in our Constitution there is an article that states that slaves are to be considered "three-fifths" of a man, which was legally valid for 78 years. Yet is it not ironic that there has never been "an unconditional apology for slavery," according to a 2014 article published in The Root. Writer Theodore R. Johnson III highlights that though the U.S. Senate and U.S. House of Representatives have drafted official apologies independently, not coming until after President Obama's election, nothing has ever been offered jointly and unconditionally. That has not stopped the United Nations from releasing a report stating America owes African-Americans reparations, and calling the policing situation a "humanitarian crisis."

At the end of the day, I have come to the point where I do not expect that there is much that will ever be done to try to atone for the effects and aftermath of slavery, Jim Crow, the War on Drugs, or police brutality in Black communities. America will never be in a place where we can compromise our fictitious position of moral superiority. (But a bigot named Trump was elected President, so who knows?) If it is not admitted to, there is always plausible deniability, which always leaves the presence of reasonable doubt. With that doubt and just enough miseducation, there is always room to dictate the narrative of what happened in the past. If any one group controls media, education, and holds legislative power they are in prime position to consistently determine how the story is told. Not saying that my education to this point was anything short of amazing, but I surely had serious and reasonable questions about the history books. And thus, we must be willing to see society for what it is and what it is not. The only hope that we have is by changing the minds of our citizens and then we can begin to see the change in how our society operates. This work is and always will be uncomfortable, but it is our duty to reclaim the best of what our society must offer. It is our mandate and our right to rebel against such a system.

RECLAIM

"The reason why the world lacks unity, and lies broken and in heaps, is, because man is disunited with himself."

–Ralph Waldo Emerson

No one was ever more important in my education career than Mr. Leroy Foster, my 8th grade history teacher, who used our history book as a reference, but who taught a secondary curriculum. He would commonly tell us what we would see on the state-mandated test, however also provided applicable context and truth about an event in history. No subject was off limits and nothing was too taboo for his class. I believe that he understood the words of famed-historian Carter G. Woodson when he said, "The so-called modern education, with all its defects, however, does others so much more good than it does the Negro, because it has been worked out in conformity to the needs of those who have enslaved and oppressed weaker peoples."

Every class seemed to have provided something groundbreaking, eye-popping, or conscious shattering and I absolutely loved it. Not because he was such a good instructor, and he was, but because it was the first time I had a Black man as an instructor, and one who told me the truth about where I came from and who I was. It was a life-changing class and one that sparked my unceasing interest in the history of two major pieces of who I am; American and Black. Nevertheless, the hard truth is that I have always been more Black than American. I have always identified more with the struggle for equal and equitable rights of people who look like me.

Someone is reading this and strongly believes that some of the statements are racist or I am exercising "reverse racism," but I am here to tell you that you are sorely mistaken. Truth or the stating of facts in no way makes you racist, and frankly does not even capture the essence of the definition. The meaning of racism is one of the most commonly misconstrued parts of all conversations about race relations. Over the course of decades, there has been this belief that those who are in the minority, about population size, political, and/or economic power, can be racist; by definition this is impossible. If you Google, the definition of racism what comes back is:

1.   The belief that all members of each race possess characteristics and abilities specific to that race, especially so as to distinguish it as inferior or superior to another race or races.

2.   Prejudice, discrimination, or antagonism directed against someone of a different race based on the belief that one's own race is superior.

Given the fact that Google is the #1 search tool globally, it would not be farfetched that there is a lot of confusion about racism. If it was as simple as a belief of inferiority or superiority, then hell FIFA or the Olympics Committee would be the most racist organizations out there. Because everyone who participates in the World Cup or Olympics believes that their country (and subsequently their race) is superior to others. So, imagine characterizing the Olympics, the greatest athletic competition for any athlete to compete in, as a racist display of athleticism instead of something that serves to unify us. If we take the definition of racism Google offers us then we can surely accept this ridiculous interpretation about the Olympics, right? Not likely, because it sounds crazy unless you believe alternative facts.

One of the determining factors for the existence of racism is power. Any race who is without the ability to alter, impede, or stifle the livelihood of another race cannot be guilty of subscribing to racism. So, all the history about the obstacles for Black people, and particularly Black males, are facts that substantiate the existence of racism in our society. This notion that is consistently perpetuated that by referencing racial history or celebrating your own history with pride is a problem is, for lack of a better term, bullshit. Just like that. I say it so definitively because I have seen on too many occasions in the media that they condemn anyone who speaks out about racial inequality.

Our, those of African descent, most celebrated historical figure is Martin King, Jr., but American history conveniently forgets that they called him a communist, socialist, and divisive when he was in the heart of his movement. A contemporary example is from the Black Lives Matter movement when people compare raising current issues about police brutality and racial profiling to racism on the part of the protestors. How can these two things possibly be equated?

The greatest lie that has been disseminated was that we lived in a post-racial America after the election of President Barack

Hussein Obama. Nothing could have been further from the truth. Over the course of his presidency, the true ugliness that is America's racial divide became more and more evident. His very presence, and the presence of his family in the White House, was enough to give birth to the darkest period of overt racial intolerance since the political upheaval of Jim Crow. Never had a governor put her finger in the face of a sitting U.S. president, a U.S. Senator call the President a liar on the floor of Congress, considerable questioning of his birth country and legitimacy of his presidency, or depictions of the President as a monkey being circulated widely. All of this in our *post-racial* society which evidently does not exist. It would be amazingly convenient for this to be true but it is not the case. It would be great to have nothing left to protest over that dehumanizes us or inhibits our progress. So, it is a safe bet to make that we, Black people in America, would not be the ones to continue or resurrect racism, right?

Yet, race is one of those taboo areas in our society that everyone walks on eggshells when discussing. It has so many nuances and is associated with so much pain and anguish for so many people. Due to its touchiness, many people struggle to even broach the subject for fear of being politically incorrect or offending someone of a different race. Yet there is little commonality, or seemingly so, about the topic, which often brings the conversation to a stalemate. When considering what racism really means with ample consideration paid to our history and its roots, I began to see a clearer picture of what it was all about. It was like a deepened revelation about what was the overarching premise that was consistent on both sides. The conundrum when it comes to race is that there is always so many deep feelings and beliefs that are associated with everyone's opinion. When was the last time you heard a fact-based, objective conversation about race with anyone not on a news program? Not likely that you ever have or it was a rare one off.

Racism was an economic imperative to the founding of the New World that was more pressing than any moral dilemmas that arose from the institution of slavery. The systematic oppression was the result of one essential goal which was, and always is, money. Money meant more economic stability to fend off attacks by other European rivals as war was rather common on the continent. In fact, there were over 100 wars between factions over land and trade in the 15th and 16th centuries. Thus, the advent of the slave trade was ignited by the need to have economic advantage over foes who were constantly seeking to conquer their and new lands. So, when we consider what has been the foundation of racism in this country, we must acknowledge these roots. So, when the New World was being stolen from indigenous peoples across the globe, there was no true malice toward them, but more greed to take what they possessed. It may not be a comfortable reality that we have, but it is the truest. Yet, the historical depiction of the events that followed were the epitome of racism.

Half-truths and flat-out lies are the basis for the social inequities that have arisen in our country's history. "Only Christopher we acknowledge is Wallace," is one of the more infamous lines from Jay-Z on his *Magna Carta Holy Grail* album and one of the most appropriate. It all starts with the longest persisting lie, which is that Christopher Columbus discovered the New World. Even though it is common knowledge that you cannot discover a place that is already inhabited, schools still teach that "...Columbus sailed the ocean blue," as if he was the epitome of a heroic liberator of savage peoples. The book that changed my entire perception of the Americas was the quintessential work that dispels myths by Ivan Van Sertima called *They Came Before Columbus: The African Presence in Ancient America.* This indictment of the historical inaccuracies of the Columbus story was powerful and revealing regarding how and why the narrative has been changed. It was essentially the maintenance of age-old misrepresentation of the contributions of minorities in world history. It can be seen in everything from portrayals of Jesus, Moses, and other Biblical characters who hail from a melanin-rich part of the world, to Ancient Kush. In movies like Gods of Egypt starring an all-white cast minus their African slaves.

Racism is a system of advantages based on race used by those with power to remain in a favorable position. This definition is the combination of the David Wellman's thoughts from *Portraits of White Racism* jazzed up by yours truly. I think it should be clearly stated and boldly championed that the idea behind racism is not to make a race of people feel bad. It is squarely about maintaining power and benefiting from its privileges. One of the oldest universally known quotes is that, "absolutely power corrupts absolutely," which has been tested thousands of times and always remains the same. Or maybe John Steinbeck said it best, "Power does not corrupt. Fear corrupts. Perhaps the fear of a loss of power." Yet, we have this constant dilemma, this persistent conundrum that it seems like nothing will ever change. There must be a significant change in the way that we address or even perceive power itself. Not saying that we should all be anarchists and wear *V for Vendetta* masks trying to topple our own government, though our very own Constitution says we have such a right. But that is impractical and frankly that type of rhetoric takes us nowhere.

For those who believe that we need to diametrically change our system of government and press the reset button on our society, I believe are naive. Not because their ideas are not valid, but because if you understood how the power structure works then you would fully grasp that the system is working as it was designed.

The one thing that will always remain the most powerful influence in our society is the constant longing for improvement. If you do not believe me then reflect on 2008 when this country elected Barack Obama. Think about all those young people who came out to vote for the first time. The emotion, the passion, the fire that burned in us was so powerful because of what we had witnessed. We witnessed our country's greatness fall to the wayside after 9-11 and were on the cusp of a financial crisis under Bush.

On the flip side of that coin, think about all the Republican voters who stayed away from the polls during that election or the next in 2012. Or those who came out or sat home to elect a reality TV star in Donald Trump this election. Remember why? It was because there was not a nominee who galvanized them or inspired them more than they perceived in their chosen candidate. It all comes from this burning and unquenchable desire that drives us all to strive for more or better. Power, and the subsequent money, that is derived from it is the foundation of what this country stands on.

Strive or Die Trying

All this conversation on race boils down to *striving* or that strong desire for you and your loved ones to live the best life possible. When looking at the persistence of racism as a method of striving, something that we all wish to attain, it becomes much easier to swallow. We all are striving for something individually or collectively within a group of people with a similar cause. Every revolution, rebellion, or movement started with striving to attain some type of equality or right. Each of us has been prescribed one life, and thus one opportunity, to make the most out of it. Therefore, when there is opposition or obstruction to that opportunity, we will do whatever is in our power to fight back. So, when you consider race or racism in America, and the tension that arises from it, we must take a step back and understand where it comes from: *striving.*

The principal issue within this universal longing to have more is the notion of *striving* is that there are always layers of opposition for those who possess less power in a society. This comes from a myriad of things including economic and political power, yet people often have differing opinions of how this happens. The idea of "pulling yourself up by your bootstraps" is one of the longest-told stories in American society. It presumes that everyone starts with an even playing field in America, and thus has the same opportunities as anyone else. That is to say that anyone can be rich or anyone can be successful as the next person regardless of who they are; this is the heart of the American meritocracy. That what you do individually is all that makes a difference to the quality of your life. That no one outside of yourself has the ability to improve or hinder your growth and success. This is a myth of the highest order and something that everyone should be willing to challenge.

"It's alright to tell a man to pull himself up by his own bootstraps, but it is cruel jest to say to a bootless man that he ought to lift himself with his own bootstraps," remarked Dr. King. And when we honestly explore the dynamics of America we must come to grips that everyone does not. It is far too convenient to believe the sentiments of Donald Trump and others who believe in racist stereotypes saying, "Laziness is a trait in blacks." That there are certain people who have a genetic predisposition to act a certain way. It is a farce; it is flat out untrue yet there is a good portion of America that attribute Black social position with our willingness to work hard. Does not that take society off the hook? Absolutely.

Whether you read *Under the Affluence* by Tim Wise or *The Case for Reparations* by Ta-Nehesi Coates or by taking a walk down any street in urban America, we all know that this is not the case. Warren Buffett, in a 2010 interview with Malcolm Forbes and Jay-Z, remarked, "If I'd been born in 1930, if I'd been born a female, if I'd been born Black, I would not have had the same opportunities that I had." In similar order, Bill Gates acknowledged his fortunate upbringing saying, "I had better exposure to software development at a young age than I think anyone in that period, and all because of an incredibly lucky series of events." A perfect example of this is when Donald Trump said that he received a "small $1,000,000 loan" from his father to start his business negating the fact that he is *beyond* privileged to be able to make such a request. So, when two of the wealthiest men in the world come to the realization that their fortune was in some ways a benefit to when they were born and the advantages they had, we should believe them.

One of the hardest things that people fail to come to grips with is their own privilege. I have seen white people in tears after reflecting and acknowledging the benefits of their own whiteness. It is not something that anyone can take lightly or be cold to because it is an absolute shock when one finally accepts that they have been the beneficiary of unfair benefits that have derived at its foundation by the oppression of minorities throughout history. One of the most powerful reflections came when a white woman, in a diversity course I helped design, had a biracial grandchild and she realized that the world is not going to be as equitable to him as it is her or her daughter, his mother.

Privilege, as described previously, is "*a special right, immunity, or exemption granted to persons in authority to free them from certain obligations or liabilities.*" I want to be clear that privilege is a byproduct of racism and that when privilege becomes more apparent, racism is often more prevalent as well. Much like God does not exist without the faith to believe in Him, white privilege does not exist without racism. Privilege is the reason for ALL the turmoil in the lives of minorities. Privilege is the reason why access is denied, deaths are justified, exploitation is celebrated, families are broken, and millions of dollars have been and are currently being stolen. I did not want to make it seem as if these things have ever stopped because they have not; the methods have simply changed. They are more covert or hidden ways to get the job done nowadays. In the hypocritical words of President Reagan, "Peace is more than just an absence of war. True peace is justice, true peace is freedom, and true peace dictates the recognition of human rights." Privilege, by design, does not force its possessor to reconcile with these ideas and strive for limitations of their prevalence. They are not called to live on the outside of the house looking in, and thus the work of unity is continuous, contentious, and frustrating.

Recognizing privilege is the first step to moving from someone who is oblivious about race and its injustices to someone who can contribute in their own way to lessen its predominance somehow. It is so deeply interwoven into our society that at times there is nothing that can be done to combat it, but that simply is not true. So, we must constantly refresh our thinking and be able to interpret things honestly.

Unpacking Bias

The history of African-Americans in this country is one of constant disappointment and discouragement. However, it is one of unbelievable perseverance and amazing feats that have been accomplished by those who were able to hold themselves to a higher standard. This belief is what formulated my bias toward Historically Black College and Universities (HBCU). It is also why I always help students enter and succeed in those spaces with so much fervor. Not because I believe that you can attain a superior education in the classroom, but I fully endorse the social curriculum that you are trained on while in attendance. The Atlanta University Center (AUC), for example, is one of those unique spaces that have a concealed curriculum that was equally important as the in-class work I received. It was the first time I realized that there were other people who were my age, who looked like me, and who had equally impressive qualifications, inspiring dreams, and passionate drive to accomplish them. Nothing was or is more encouraging than knowing that I am not alone on my grind to make significant change in the world.

Most importantly, I concluded that there was something intangible about an HBCU that was intentional about teaching me about myself, as well as showing me how to navigate the world around me as a Black man. Regardless of the quality of education, if you do not cultivate the intangible skills that make you an asset in any situation you will always be expendable. So, when people ask me was my $140,000 degree worth it to attend Morehouse, I emphatically say," Yes it was!" Not because I had a great paying job upon graduation or any other superficial reason admissions counselors try to sell you on. The education was worth it for the network of people that I love, the same network that constantly pushes me forward, and the knowledge of self that was expanded. Morehouse provided clarity on the difference between sustainable progress and superficial, temporary growth. So, when it comes to the underlying premise of this book it has been invaluable. There would be no Carlton, as the world knows him, without that school on a red clay hill in Georgia.

There are certain moments in every person's life that require the utmost attention and resolve to make it through with a sound mind. These fractions of time carry the distinction and burden that can alter your life's course transforming the individual for better or worse. It is in these times that each soul must ask the burning question of "what's truly important in my life?" This simple, yet remarkably powerful, inquiry opens the proverbial floodgates to understanding of self and one's ever-changing journey toward a sustainable living. It lies at the basis of ever career, relationship, emotion, and decision every person engages with daily. It has been known to silence titanic figures and quiet unruly spirits with its profound simplicity. It only desires composed, peaceful reflection. It demands calculated introspection for it is definitive. It is essential to finding harmony.

A popular quote states, "that you make time for what you care about," and I would agree. Yet, I do not believe this takes its intended message far enough. This has been grossly overused and consistently distorted to evoke emotion and to arouse what are deemed appropriate behaviors in a relationship. Yet, there is absence of consideration for the condition of the person this is addressed towards. Whenever one fails to realize that emotionally charged situations have unforeseen layers of complexity, there will always be disservice done to all those involved. This is evident in the countless instances of mistaken interpretation or unnecessary demonstrative reactions to seemingly harmless conversation.

For we never know the depth of one's linkage to misfortune or their union to pain. Thus, we should be unassuming in our quest for clarity and devoid of prejudice to truly be empathetic toward another's suffering. We have a mandate to our fellow man to see him or her as they are and not what we wish them to be. Freedom from the shackles of bias is the key to developing one's pallet for equitable analysis of the world around them.

Bias, in its simplest form, is defined as "a belief in one way; partiality toward someone or something," which serves as the foundation toward a parochial or short-sighted view. It is the basis for what is convenient in someone's life. The thing about biases is that they never force you to push the envelope. They allow you to continue to stay in your "safety" zone without any additional bother. Without pressure to change it up or to make a different decision. You have what you like and you stick with what you know.

The troubling thing about living solely by your biases is that there is very little room for growth. You stay in this inhibiting cycle of convenience that limit your opportunities for newness. It constrains your ability to make considerable, permanent change in your life that brings fresh experiences. It leaves you frozen in place awaiting miraculous transformation to make life...invigorating once more. This is not the life that one can imagine living. It is not one that people spend their lives longing for. It is certainly not one that people prayed on bended knee about.

One of my favorite sermons by T.D. Jakes highlighted God's grace, defined as "unmerited favor," and what outsiders are going to think about your life when they see it moving positively. It all came to a head when he tagged the sermon as "Favor Ain't Fair." It was masterfully written and beautifully articulated, but it also offered so much clarity to this discussion on bias. When it comes to bias, we must be willing to accept that we will often land on the wrong side of it. No one will always end up on the positive side of someone's biases. It does not have to be fair or equitable, or even positive, because we cannot control anyone else's upbringing or thought life.

Throughout the course of your life, you will find that people make the same decisions repeatedly. Most of the time they make these decisions without any considerable thought. The fuel for bias is simple: instinctual thinking. Whenever we use our instincts, which operate within our subconscious mind, we will always lean toward what is familiar. Whenever we use analysis and objectivity (as much as possible), we are basing our decision-making off our conscious and rational thoughts. We must learn to be more aware of this process and we should be open to the idea of experiencing more than what we are accustomed to.

According to The Royal Society's 2015 YouTube video, Understanding Unconscious Bias, there are four critical steps that can be taken to ensure that you are not operating instinctually all the time. These are: 1) Deliberately slow down decision-making; 2) Reconsider reasons for decisions; 3) Question cultural stereotypes; 4) Monitor each other for unconscious bias. This ongoing and potent process of continuous reflection is one that will make you stronger with each rational, positive decision you make. Whenever I move into a new position or take part of some new process, I always make one simple request: Tell me everything. I love to have all the facts before I start my analysis into what are the best possible steps to achieve the goal. I suggest that you do the same. Consider all the details and follow the process to make the best decision; convenience be damned. To be successful in this world, you must be willing to shed convenience. As previously stated, nothing grows in comfortable. So, when it comes to conversation about race, we must be willing to be uncomfortable if we are ever going to grow as a country.

With the election of Donald Trump as President of the United States of America, we have four long years to be in a constant state of discomfort. We must embrace that. We must be comfortable with being uncomfortable. Do we still need to be open to listening to each other and understand their perspective? Absolutely we must, but that is not possible if we allow fear to force us to be stagnant. Former Attorney General Eric Holder once spoke on race relations remarking, "People feel uncomfortable talking about racial issues out of fear that if they express things, they will be characterized in a way that is not fair. I think that there is still a need for a dialogue about things racial that we've not engaged in."

So today, we are faced with a new challenge of being able to share our thoughts and feelings without allowing our biases to control our language. When the time comes, we must be willing to commit ourselves to the process of thinking without overt bias.

Fear Not the Journey

Fear is the central player, the key component, in this tense, aggravated relationship between Black males and police. Fear that officers have of Black males, who are perceived to be more violent and more criminally inclined, against the fear that every officer is crooked, trigger-happy, and dedicated to the "taking of black bodies," in the words of famed author and writer Ta-Nehisi Coates. The gulf between these opposing vantage points is drastic, yet they have a common denominator, which is safety. When you consider Maslow's Hierarchy of Needs, there are physiological needs, which are the base of the pyramid quickly followed by safety needs. After you have food, shelter, and clothing, the next essential need is to feel safe, which is hard to come by in the world of over-policing and reliance on the underground economy. Jay-Z put it this way, "Whoever said illegal was the easy way out couldn't understand the mechanics and the workings of the underworld." So, imagine the intense strain that is placed on the hearts and minds of men in these chosen or forced illicit professions.

When you listen to an officer speak about what is the most important aspect of his/her day, you commonly hear a response that references making it back home after a shift. Their job, their very role in society is predicated on the idea that they are tasked to deal with any and everything that comes their way. They cannot (or should not) be dispassionate about one dispatch and fired up about the next. Every single day they perform their jobs as admirably as possible while grappling with the reality that today may be their final day. This is the EXACT same existence for those who have been confined to the underground economy and who come from impoverished beginnings. The similarities are so essential to understand and serves as seemingly the only place where deep wounds can begin to mend.

It is critical to note that there is a shared experience that should be acknowledged for any semblance of reconciliation to be possible. That shared experience or bias is one of survival by any means necessary. It may be clouded on both ends by fear, but its essence is singular and very clear. Both the criminal and the cop wish to see tomorrow. Yet, the major difference is that there was a choice that could be made by the officer and not much of one available to the criminal, or at least not one their survival allowed time for. Much like their authoritative counterpart, the criminal in an urban community is also given the responsibility to deal with whatever comes his way. No matter the pain that comes with it or the desperation, anxiety, or angst it causes, it must be dealt with. I should be clear that there is no difference in the mentality that must be taken to survive a day as an officer versus a day in a life of a criminal. The major exception to these two experiences is that one is paid with an expectation to survive and the other survives with the hope to be paid. The gulf or division between these factions is a matter of economics not values.

As an advisor and mentor to so many young people over the past decade, I cannot and do not advocate for anyone to stray from the pathways that education offer; it is "the great equalizer of the conditions of men," according to Horace Mann. But I have seen that a student cannot focus on his school work if he has no food in his stomach, and cannot do homework if there are no lights when he gets home. I have seen the effects on one's education when their life experience does not align with their school involvement. Daniel

Pink noted, "You have to not be struggling for survival. For people who do not know where their next meal is coming, notions of finding inner motivation are comical." Even Maslow would contend that it is natural that they seek to meet their physiological needs first by any means at their disposal.

Unfortunately, in impoverished communities, this tends to be in the form of illegal substances that are readily available and the risk of imprisonment, or even death, pale in comparison when faced with survival. Knowing the feeling of not having a roof over my head, if only for a night, or not knowing where my next meal would come from was enough to do whatever was necessary to survive, if only for a little while. America and its (in)justice system must come to a peaceful understanding that this is the reality for the most heavily-policed, under-resourced urban areas in our country. Crime is not a byproduct of race or ethnicity but an intended consequence of poverty coupled with substantially fewer options for financial stability.

When we discuss the act of rebellion, we must be clear about its definition and positive about its implications. An act of rebellion does not mean, in all cases, that violence is always associated with it. It means most potently now in the 21st century that you take back control over your relationships. We all know that first impressions last forever in most cases, nevertheless we rarely think about what it takes to better handle it. We must be intentional about managing, even the minute details of our relationships particularly those with acquaintances. The relationships with those people who are not close with you are the ones that are predicated on a surface level until they get to know you better. Our society is based heavily on the superficial and unless you deal with this reality, you will allow limitations to be placed on yourself.

As mentioned before you cannot own the biases that people have, but you can challenge intolerance that exists from people who do not share similar cultural backgrounds. In my case, Black males have a serious issue to deal with regarding public perception. I cannot change the media portrayal, but I can command my appearance. Not saying that you should have to change to be your natural self, but I am saying that you must learn to play the game. By playing the game, you can win it. If you decide that you do not want to play, then you will constantly struggle to progress in life. No one is at fault for this, but it is the way the cookie crumbles. You must be willing to see the long-game and not simply the short-term impacts. All of that begins and ends with the recognition that you must be conscious of your behavior.

Prescription for Action

To rebel, you must reflect on your habits and how you have been conditioned to behave. I should be aware of the biases that are naturally in place that I must deal with, but also have a strategy to combat them. Rebel (v): deliberate behavior formulated and perceived as constructive interaction that transforms relations with another being. So, to rebel is to be positive and to be resolute and to be solution-oriented. All I know how to do is be solution-oriented, and consequently I believe that my very existence should offer a counter-narrative to what people believe about young Black males.

The way I talk in professional circles, the way I dress, the way I handle business, and the way I pursue my goals are all intentional. To be deliberate is the first step, because then you can be pointed, laser-focused until it becomes part of your daily walk. To be a person who masters relationships, you must be willing to dictate the terms. By thinking before you open your mouth to speak and being solution-oriented, you will be shaping what others think of you. You will have the ability to determine the outcome of the conversation before it ever starts.

There is a serious need to always want to say the perfect thing. I cannot remember how many times I was shot down by a young lady I approached. There was always something that I could have done better in hindsight. But after a while, I had to realize that it was not my forte. I had to stay in my wheel house, which was developing genuine and organic relationships. If you ask anyone who knows me they will tell you that I never enjoyed approaching women. I did it so I would not get capped on, but never took pleasure in it. Maybe I was too self-conscious or maybe I just realized that I needed something more substantive. Either way, I knew that the way that relationships were formed made all the difference to how they were built and how they were sustained.

Anytime you are trying to build something you must start with a strong foundation, that is why I am so optimistic about my marriage. The strong foundation, when it comes to interacting with other people, is to be deliberate and constructive. If you can do those two things, you always have a chance to form endearing relationships, or at least leave people with a positive impression. Your reputation is something that, in most cases, will meet people before you ever physically do. You can bet your bottom dollar that there is someone out there willing to report on whatever positive, and especially negative perceptions that they have of you. In the case of any rebel, you should be meticulous in your approach to every situation where you are going to meet new people. You must have a methodology in place.

Networking is the life bread of the world we live in today for several different reasons, but none more important than the fact that your name should mean something. There are plenty of nobodies in this world who do not want anything and who cannot imagine doing anything substantial. I refuse to believe that someone who wants the best out of life can accomplish that without building a network.

At Morehouse, they tell us that, "we pay for the name and the network," and I took that to heart. I had to learn how to navigate new and terrifying waters at times, but the key was to *always be constructive* or ABC. I could meet so many people and have access to so much, because I always made myself an asset, and not a liability, to have around. If I could make an elders' life just a little bit easier, I would do so. If I could connect a friend with a resource that I had access to, I would without provocation. On the movie Layer Cake, the egotistical villain stated after positioning himself favorably that, "The best businessman is a great middle man." I used that philosophy in reference to my network of like-minded people. I believe that the best friend to have is a great connector.

So, as we bring this section to a close, we must acknowledge that there are biases that others have that will always be out of our control. We need to have clarity on the idea, that in the conversation on race in America, that we should find commonality. We must know that the way we present ourselves is how people will come to know us. There are plenty of reasons and anomalies to these statements, but the reality is that we cannot prepare for those. We should know that people are out here doing their best to understand this wild world that we live in. We must be comfortable with the realization that everyone is not going to be able to control their biases.

You should be positive that if you know how to offer solutions that people will see you as an asset. Nothing is absolute in this world nor will it ever be, but we must know what it is that we have control over and do our best to perfect that. We must be determined to master where we are presently at, to leverage it for our future growth and success. Awareness without clarity of how to operationalize it offers little more than general knowledge. Awareness plus clarity opens the heavens of consciousness and self-awareness that will help you reach your next level. That is how this all works. That is how this has always worked. Join the solution or live hazardously as the problem.

REDEFINE

"We are all trying to get to this next level without the next level finding us."

-Lauryn Hill

We have the fortune and burden of living in times that censorship does not exist anymore to any great extent. Everyone has their own podium and stage where they can share with the world who they are and what they believe. Free speech has never been wielded so liberally to the masses as it has become with social media. Social media has been changing the world for better, and for always, in ways that no one could have ever imagined. It has become this unstoppable vehicle used by anyone who is bold or courageous enough to share their vision with the world.

It, in many ways, has parallels with some of the greatest creative movements of people throughout history. It can be compared to the Renaissance in the 14th Century, because of what it did to change the thoughts and minds of people who were in place to experience it. The major difference this time is that technology has brought us so far that we are unbelievably connected to each other in ways that our ancestors, or even our elders, were not. We truly live in a global society and everything that happens online can be seen across the world by an astronomical amount of people. Even more, once something is put online by or about you, it lives forever in the vastness of the Internet. This reality has already and will continue to shape and reshape our world until we build a truly global interconnected community.

Atmosphere of Change

This connectedness began for me back in 1996 when I was in the second grade in Ms. Cornelius' class at Lincoln Heights Missionary Baptist Christian Academy. Back in the day, second grade meant you were learning how to write complete sentences, more advanced arithmetic, develop your understanding of money, and many other foundational lessons, but for our class we were introduced to computers. In fact, I have a fond place in my heart for Apple because of this; we were using Macintosh computers, which was by far the coolest thing about school to that point. I still remember the excitement when it was "computer time," and we had to follow along with the teacher as she taught a lesson using it.

By that time, I was an avid user of Nintendo, which was played daily with games like Super Mario Brothers, Duck Hunt, and Track & Field (with the running mat included). So, technology itself was not brand new to me, but this was the first time I saw utility in it. Very few people had computers at home, as it was a luxury item in those days. I am explaining all of this to express just how far we have come since the advent of computers. It has been an amazing period of transition for us to experience over these last 20 years, and I appreciate being on the ground floor of that transformation; it is what separates us from older generations.

My parents, much like all parents were in those days, did not allow us to live our childhoods in front of the TV playing video games. We had allotted times when we could play on Nintendo Family Computer, Sega Genesis, or PlayStation respectively, and the rest of the time was spent outside playing with friends and utilizing our imagination. The only universal rule that all kids who grew up with concerned parents had was to "be in the house by the time the street light came on." Outside of that small demand, our imaginations were our greatest and most used resource we had available. Long story short, times have changed significantly from my childhood to now. The youth born anytime in the last 7-10 years are considered to be digital natives, "a person born or brought up during the age of digital technology and therefore familiar with computers and Internet from an early age." This was not the experience with any generation until now, and as a result some of the age-old rules that were passed onto us are no longer applicable in the same way. Parents no longer must only manage their child's physical environment, but must the worry about their social environment via the web. It makes it so much harder to be a parent nowadays as you can imagine. And It has never been more imperative to make sure each child knows who he or she is for themselves. Far too many of my students are defined by the opinions and perceptions of their peers.

We live in times that are more diverse, freer, more optimistic, and more unsheltered than ever before, but there is a flipside to this truth. Everyone in developed countries has access to smartphones, multiple social media outlets, Wi-Fi internet, and a camera at all times. It has been the greatest shift in culture that has ever happened in such a short period of time. The Renaissance spanned the better part of four centuries and changed the world, but the digital revolution has been a widespread movement for less than 20 years. Steve Jobs made it his life's work to put a personal computer or PC in every home starting in 1977, but it did not become a reality for most until the late 90s or early 2000s. Things are moving at an astronomical pace and there is nothing that can be done to slow it down at this point. Why? Because it was not always like this, not even close.

Once upon a time, what came on the nightly news and in the morning paper was the ultimate source of information for the masses. This was a time that society, and subsequently mainstream culture, was influenced greatly by titanic figures in the only form of approved media and information sharing. That no longer is our reality, because there are millions of different sources and perspectives that are shared with the world on an hourly basis that are now the social influencers. The culture has shifted so much that even our trending topics are making the nightly news now. This has led to a new industry that is so contrary to what we once knew that it has even changed our protests and has disrupted censorship altogether.

In years past, if there was something too controversial or did not align with the values of the TV station, or even the person in charge it would not see the light of day. For example, we would have never seen the death of dozens of Black males throughout the country on the news, and subsequent nationwide protests, if it was not for our newfound access. To be honest, the ground-breaking passage into law of gay marriage would not have been possible either. Even more, we would not have had the first Black president in Barack Obama elected had it not been for his prowess with social media. Our generation does not care about whether something said is politically correct anymore, but whether it is socially appropriate.

One of the most important affirmations I received as a kid when I was headed out of the house into an unfamiliar place and my father reminded me that, "Your last name is Collins and that I represent all of us everywhere that you go." It was something that always kept me in line throughout the years whenever I got the idea to do something incredibly stupid even as an adult. It was not that I was a bad child or that I always acted out, but rather that it needed to be reinforced that there was something greater than myself at work in my actions. So, for this generation of youth, who live their lives through the digital world, it is imperative that they have a similar understanding that their actions have consequences that have a ripple effect on their personal brand (particularly if it is one that they did not construct themselves). There has never been a higher need for personal accountability in our everyday lives since what we do now has a digital footprint and lives forever on the web. When I was in college, we made it a point to never allow our picture to be captured doing terribly inappropriate or socially unacceptable behavior, because we knew that it would follow us. It has paid off tremendously over the years when I was asked to share my social media profiles with employers and others in my network. More importantly, it was a consciousness that was so necessary for my development as a productive adult. We understood that our actions today impacted our future and the future of our children by default. This was the responsibility that I was forced to bare. But there are rules that had to be followed for me to prosper.

An Elevated Perspective

In my lifetime, I have seen people succeed and others fail for a variety of reasons, but most often it was because they were unable to leave their life of convenience. There was something so intoxicating about the way they went about their everyday life that they refused to adapt to change. I have seen some of the most talented people I have ever met fail miserably because they held onto people and poor habits for far too long. Remember that there is a time and place for everything, but more importantly that everyone cannot travel with you on all your voyages in life; nor should they. We must be willing to sacrifice whatever is keeping us from the greatest version of ourselves. It is our personal responsibility that we must completely own.

During our lives, we all develop biases and prejudices that contribute to our overall outlook on life. Yet, we must be able to harness them for our benefit and ensure that they do not come back to harm us later. We must be able to discern what will and will not obstruct future progress in our lives. It requires a certain amount of privilege and wealth to be able to simply forget the opinions of other people. This privileged mindset is usually reserved for the top 10% of the top 1% of our society. For everyone else, we should remain aware of what it is that can negatively impact our lives.

A perfect example is Donald J. Trump, who is regretfully President of the United States. He has found a way to consistently share hateful, divisive, misogynistic, racist, and narcissistic messaging that has impacted his public perception forever. But that does not matter to him because he is a billionaire. As a billionaire, you have all the leeway in the world to make whatever incendiary comments you want. His supporters on the other hand have not been so fortunate.

Many Trump supporters have found themselves in hot water because of their racist or sexist statements they have made. This often happens by repeating or continuing a line of thought that came from their candidate. There are plenty of examples of people who have been fired for their remarks, because they falsely believed that they were above reproach. That is not the America that we live in any longer. We should come to grips with reality and succumb to the idea that there are rules to the game we play. There is always a part of the privileged class that believes that they are above decorum, or just generally morality, but most cannot afford to think that way. As much as social media has benefited our lives, it has also ruined many others' because they did not keep their biases in check. Everything you think should not see the light of day, if it does you will have to atone for the thoughtlessness with lost relationships, respect, and/or resources.

When we stop and consider all the negative or contentious things said about President and First Lady Obama in their years in office or Hillary on the campaign trail, we should take pause and wonder where it all comes from. We should question what we thought to be a sensible and logical nation. We must challenge what has been rationalized and the thought process that went into accepting some of this hateful speech. It gets frustrating, at times, to even think about the depths of where most of the hatred comes from. We simply go back and forth with much of the lunacy trying to understand what cannot be explained. Much of it are thoughts that have never dissipated, they simply remained underground. Trump became an excuse to let what many have thought all along to come out and be shared boldly. The rhetoric that has been spewed by these passionate political critics, and that has been covered mercilessly by CNN, MSNBC, and others for ratings, has been terrible. Yet, we must accept that there is plenty more of this to go around. This is only the dawn of a dark day (four long years) in American history.

As a person donning the race of the group in which most attacks are aimed, I can say that I should have some feelings of despair or disillusionment; I do not. I have been conditioned, to this point, to set my expectations of popular culture and of the dominant class in America very low. Unfortunately, Trump continues to lower those expectations, but funny thing is that I appreciate him so much for doing so. I feel like our society has needed someone like him for quite some time. He has forced conversations about race relations, religious freedom, gender equality, and financial inequity that would not have been possible without his deeply angry, fear-stirring speeches. He has opened many naïve eyes to the underbelly of our country that has been mostly hidden, and discounted...for decades. It was common for people to dismiss a racist as a "bad egg" or an "anomaly," but with Trump as our elected leader, we cannot attribute it to anything but what it is: Racist White America.

We should offer The Donald a Nobel Peace Prize for this

work that he is doing 150 years post-Civil War. He has placed a significant spotlight on the overt racism that we have been overlooking for so long. This type of division will force our country to reunite in ways that we could not have anticipated. He has presented us with an opportunity that could scarcely have been realized without his chauvinistic and bigoted bombast. All of this is to say that we, as a country, have some ugly truths and beautiful lies that we must address if we are going to move forward genuinely addressing equity. There are so many biases, prejudices, and inequitable situations that have remained unchecked for far too long. But the solution to this problem is, and always will begin with, the citizenry, and more importantly the sole individual willing to stand for something more than self-preservation.

Since the 2015-2016 school year, I participated in and facilitated sessions for a diversity conversation with fellow educators in Cincinnati that have been extremely positive. We have had discussions on everything from race to bias to equity and everything in between. What came of all the talks was that we are all different people with very differing ideas of what the world has to offer us. It was often split along racial and socioeconomic lines, but it was always enriching. It gave an opportunity to share my thoughts with white people and for them to offer their perspective in return. It was the most open and intimate conversation I have had about these topics in my entire life, and my high school was the most diverse in Cincinnati. From these conversations also came the clarity that there is not a built-in aptitude to understand the politics of diversity, equity, and inclusion.

Though not everyone has had the luxury of finding a safe space to discuss sensitive topics, we all have the capacity to make a change in our approach or in what we allow from our contemporaries. We all have the ability to challenge what we have thought and what we choose to believe. Particularly if we are making an earnest and honest attempt to combat personal ignorance. This ignorance is little more than seeking the opinions of people who are not naturally in our personal or professional circles. No one, in 21st century American society, should be totally comfortable only seeking the advice of people who make things comfortable for them. (Remember nothing grows there.)

No human being grows emotionally, mentally, or spiritually without conflict. It would have been easy to say that we will maintain our usual affiliations and keep getting our usual results. If you are okay with this level of complacency then no one can stop you, but it is not something that I can ever endorse. There is too much splendor in this world to be trapped by the same four walls of the house I am already familiar with. I must venture out and be willing to accept the ugly truths and challenge the beautiful lies that this world has attempted to sell all of us.

If you are a minority in this country and do not have the ability to interact with people of other races, particularly those of the dominant race in our society, then you will always struggle to sustain yourself. We, Black people, have always been taught that if you want to be successful that you must code switch. You cannot act the same way as you do in the 'hood while you are in a corporate building. You must be able to handle yourself with the utmost professionalism and develop your camouflage.

It is hilarious when one of my students sees me away from the school environment. They are shocked at my use of slang and colorful language, which is just as much part of my personality as the professional educator. Unfortunately, my public face growing up depended on my ability to operate as if I did not care about my future. I see this now with my students and I have found that it exemplifies their inability to have the internal strength to stand alone. This is their survival technique to not stand out from the crowd as if failure is the only way to persevere; quite the contrary is the truth. Their livelihood in the future depends on my capacity to activate professionalism on-demand. These are the rules of the game that we are forced to play. No one is exempt.

On December 15, 2014, I stepped foot for the first time into Norwood High School. I was thrust into a position that I never thought was *still* possible. I entered a high school where I was the only Black faculty or staff member in the school. There was a moment of pure distress when I realized that this would be my existence for the foreseeable future. There was a fear that I would somehow be inadequate, or that I would be ostracized. I had not realized that I was trained and ready for this scenario. Given my temperament, education, upbringing, and focus on youth I knew that I would be able to handle whatever I faced in that district. I feel I was more nervous about the checkered past of the community that the school resided in. It was a very strange feeling to never culturally identify with any of my coworkers. Even worse, I felt terrible for the students of color who, before my arrival and after my departure, had no one to identify with.

When I first started driving my dad told me that there are three communities that I had to always be careful driving through as a Black young man. This was like a "birds and the bees" type of speech that is designed for your benefit, but based squarely on the Black experience in Cincinnati. The first community was Green Hills, the second was Indian Hill, and the final one was Norwood. He told me that there was a strong possibility that I would be harassed by police and that there was no reason to subject myself to that; so, stay away.

So, every day I walked into Norwood, I carried the weight of knowing the city had a past with serious racial undertones. Nonetheless, I knew that that could not impact my work or change my perspective of what needed to be done to change the lives of the young people I was charged to serve. Regardless of how I felt, I had to be a professional first and a Black man second. I had to focus on the young people in front of me and never even acknowledge the insensitive remarks that I often overheard from my office.

One of the scariest things about code switching is the possibility that you may lose yourself mid-performance. You quite possibly may forget how to be your authentic self when you constantly must show only one side of your personality. The one side that I showed was more than necessary for survival, because a socially aware Black male in a majority space is always perceived as a troublemaker until proven otherwise. So, I kept quiet to preserve my own sanity, I remained silent for the sake of the students that I was there to serve. It may come across as a selfish or cowardly act, but I also had to account for who I was in the building. I was a beacon of light for the minority students present. I was there only representation and the way that I handled every day, every task, and every challenge was going to set the tone for them. It was going to challenge unfounded beliefs about people who looked like me. It was going to set the stage for whomever came behind me. I felt as if I had to only share a component of who I am because I was the protector of the future of minorities in Norwood City Schools.

Not being able to control my thoughts and actions in this moment would have been a catastrophe waiting to happen. It would have inhibited my ability to make a difference. It would have stifled my opportunity for growth. I knew it was not the place or time to try to influence the minds of my coworkers in any way outside of my work with students. More importantly, I would have placed a glass, no better still, a concrete ceiling above my head from that point forward. The question, in these moments, is about the amount of strength you personally must possess to withstand trouble for the greater good. People think it was weak to have been nonviolent in the 1960s at the height of the Civil Rights Movement, but it was by standing still and absorbing the beatings that they were able to leave an indelible mark on our society. I am not claiming that by being in Norwood in any way compares to their struggle, I am simply stating that the thought process was the same. It was about keeping my mind in the sky regardless if I was standing in the proverbial dirt.

When we speak of the great social experiment in America

called meritocracy, we are referring to the ability to "pull yourself up by your bootstraps" and make something of your life... independently. We have already debunked this myth, but we still must address what exactly will allow for us to continually uplift ourselves. The answer is in the definition of level that was created specifically for the rebel. It reads: *Level (n): the result of consistent accomplishment that provides new opportunity for advancement.* There is so much that should be unloaded in this definition, yet it is very simple: 1) Outcomes are based on consistency; 2) Growth in life is tied to accomplishment; 3) Opportunities can only be capitalized on by those who are prepared for them; 4) Advancement is only possible when all the are in alignment. To progress in our society and climb social and economic ladders, you must be dedicated to proper positioning.

It is natural to believe that the stars do not align often in your favor, but I have come to find out that that has more to do with your perception than reality. We each have various aspects of our lives that require maintenance. We all should be willing to pay attention to the small details in our lives. We must take total control over where we are positioned and what we must do to continue to grow too big for that position. All of this is tied to navigation in many ways, as we must plan what it is that we are doing to get where we want to go. (Side note: If you do not have a destination that seems unattainable and unreachable, then you are not challenging yourself enough to seek greatness.) So, when we discuss positioning, we already assume that you are pushing yourself to the limits of your capacity. If you do not have that level of intensity, then you are your own worst enemy. No one can ever be to blame for your lack of resolve to rise in life. No passion and no purpose equates to no growth and no elevation; always has, always will. Imagine a mountain climber who is afraid of heights. Sounds crazy, right? Well, so does a person who does not believe that they can reach greater heights when it is within their capacity to do so. Winners never quit on themselves.

Let us be clear, success is for everyone, but it is not for everybody because everybody does not champion excellence. Everybody is not meant to be a rebel, someone who defies odds and hurdles obstacles. Everybody does not aspire to go higher or desire to dream bigger than their circumstance. Do not worry they will be right where you left them. You made the decision to demand better for your life and will be rewarded for it.

When we talk about getting to your next level, we know unequivocally that it will require for you to leave others behind. "I got rich and gave back to me that's the win-win," remarked Jay-Z on one of his many classics. You must be willing to elevate without feeling remorseful that you survived. You must know that you did it for the greater good. That you did it because you were a rebel at heart and success was the only way to be true to yourself. Success, when you embrace being a rebel, is the only way for you to love yourself. Elevation to your next level is a byproduct of that self-love and an appreciation for your God-given talents.

REBEL's Equation

"The way to Heaven is ascending; we must be content to travel uphill, though it be hard and tiresome, and contrary to the natural bias of our flesh."

-Jonathan Edwards

Not everyone is born with the choice to control what happens to them, around them, or privileged to not have to feel all the same growing pains in life; we know this. We also know that asking why or questioning absolute fact is a useless waste of your valuable time. Lastly, we know that there is a need for individuals to break away from the norms of society to become rebels. But we know that everyone will not answer this call; nor should they. It requires a level of simplistic mastery of a very few principles to reach the level of consciousness that will allow for your very existence to be an act of rebellion. It is a place where success is more than material wealth or possessions, but it is an expectation, almost a high calling. When you hear the call, you will know without question what it is. When it sounds an alarm, you react almost instinctively. When it is relentless, it raises your sense of urgency. It is the greatest advantage we, the self-assured rebel, has at our disposal because it is solely ours.

"I remember being blind to it/Until the day I put my mind to it/Pen and pad on the dresser for me to fine tune it/ I sat in the corner, made up my mind... DO IT!" For all the hip-hop heads out there, they know this comes from the opening of Rich Forever by Rick Ross, but for me it was more than just lyrics; it spoke directly to my soul. I listen to it now and it still brings those feelings of hunger, on second thought, of a starving recent grad doing my best to survive in Atlanta. Ironic thing about survival is that it demands so much from you that it is hard at times to find refuge in anything but the grind. The principal issue with this is that there can never be a balance in the way that your life operates. It cannot exist because survival does not allow for that luxury. Pain is a persistent symptom of this kind of lifestyle, but you should numb yourself in order to transcend to the next level.

It was my experience in this time of my life that I could not afford to feel anything that life threw at me. Whether it be brief stints of homelessness, not knowing when my next meal would come, or the pride that refused willing assistance, I felt as if I had to do it alone. There is a quality that can only be gained in life when you make it to the other side of a life-changing struggle. No matter the trial, regardless of the length or breadth, there is something uniquely magical about the ability to persevere. The journey, also known as the beautiful struggle, is such an integral part of the life of anyone who has been fortunate enough for life to demand more from them. Essentially, it is this quality which develops what the world commonly refers to as "grit" nowadays. It serves as the great internal equalizer in today's social climate.

There is a certain resilience that comes from living a life of discomfort, and it is something that can never be taken away. Something that can be perceived as commonplace for those who come from privilege can be quite the feat for someone who has far fewer means. Yet, this ability to fight for the achievement and strive tirelessly toward the accomplishment is the essence of that person's character. The internal fortitude to make something from nothing, to manifest opportunity from despair, is something that can never be taught, but rather instilled. It was something about watching those around me struggle or forcefully strive for something better in their lives that made me hunger for growth. There is something honorable about continuing the struggle for progress that my forefathers were a part of. It is this, after all, that made the difference in my life, though I never understood it growing up.

One of the most significant mantras that I use to dictate the methodology of my life is to, Live Without Regret (as much as possible). Regardless of what happens, how it occurred, or the consequences of your action or inaction, we all have the responsibility to bravely live with the outcome. When discussing my tumultuous journey to get to this place in life, I am often asked what I would change about it? This is a question that greatly amuses me because it is one that neglects to acknowledge that I would not be in this place without the struggle that brought me here. If I had not had Elijah, I would have likely never written this book or had the same sense of urgency to impact those around me. I would have been on a completely different trajectory, which would have likely included study abroad and internships in college and far less chance of coming back to Cincinnati post-grad. I would have never been able to touch the lives of dozens of young men and encourage them to venture into education. I would have never had contact with my mentees and helped them with their process to and through college. Or maybe I would have.

Do you see where this rabbit hole leads? I surely hope so. We do not have time for fantasy and conjecture about the *what if* and the *what could have been*. Your life is your life. And there is nothing that can be done to change where it has led, but everything can be done to determine where you are to go from here. In the Good Book, it tells you "do not conform to the patterns of the world," but most importantly it says that you can "be transformed with the renewing of your mind." Another translation of this calls it, "the attitude of your mind," which I believe hits closer to home for our understanding of what we must do as rebels to make the necessary changes in our lives. It does not matter what happened in your past, if you have gained something significant from the experience. I always say that "either I win or I learn," but under no circumstance do I ever see myself as a loser. My mind will not allow me to believe that I can view anything that has happened as anything less than a signal. A signal that I should be more vigilant, more aware, and better prepared for the possibility of a misstep.

Maxwell Maltz said these words, "You make mistakes. Mistakes don't make you." Nothing could be a more succinct way to say that you can never emotionally, mentally, or psychologically internalize the mishaps that occur in your life. If you do, you will have such an uphill battle to climb to get to a healthy mental space to appreciate the struggle that exists. I would say that one of my biggest and most profound supports in this effort has always been my faith in God and my belief in His covering on my life. I have repeatedly said, "I am here for an expressed purpose and if I ever stop serving His will, God no longer has reason for me to be alive." I have this immovable faith that believes that everything happens for a reason that: 1) I can immediately have understand or can rationalize in some way or; 2) I am not meant to understand yet, and must continue to be faithful to receive my answer. Either way, I live a life of complete and unwavering contentment that leads to a very sound mental life.

Notwithstanding, I would never claim that I do not have my moments of sorrow or sadness or comparison of my life to others, etc., but I always bounce back. As an individual that has used nearly every vice available at various times in life to drown sorrow and discontent, I can tell you it helps immensely to have something to believe in. It is even more beneficial when what you have to believe in is yourself. It is never as simple as an Eric Thomas motivational video or soul-stirring sermon makes it seem to inspire self-belief nor will it ever be. This is not meant to discourage you, but to simply inform you that no matter what anyone says there is a gradual process that everyone must go through.

One major thing struck me when a business partner of mine asked the question of, "Who am I to share my knowledge? What gives me the right to instruct others on what to do?" This was a very profound question and it challenged me greatly for a couple minutes until it dawned on me that I was myself. That was the only qualification that I needed, the only validation that was required. Why? Because I survived. I overcame my struggles when so many others had not, and I have been gifted with the ability to tell the story. Now there are people who would classify this arrogant or cocky (if you know anything about my alma mater, Morehouse College, then you would say this is something that is commensurate with our kind lol), but there is nothing vain about this belief. It is simply a deeper understanding that I do not have to compare myself to others, but rather I must value my own experience. I must value it enough to believe that it can be used to help others. That it can be used as a tool for positivity and motivation.

As a devoted Christian and follower of the teachings of the Bible I believe the words of James 4:17 which states, "Anyone who knows the good he ought to do and doesn't do it, sins." I see it as my greatest responsibility to positively impact the world around me and transform the life of every young person that I encounter. It is something that I consciously devote myself to and feel that it is the calling that has been placed on my life.

In fact, I am bound to do so by a promise I made back in 2007 to my grandfather, post-mortem, who made it possible to attend my college of choice. It was through every experience that Reverend Robert Russell Collins and Betty Jean Collins immersed us in, inside and outside of the church, that opened our eyes to a vast world of opportunity. It changed what I believed was possible. When my partner asked that question it called for a thorough reflection on what enables the belief that I can be something greater than myself. Before we dig any deeper, I want to leave you with something to ponder, "Who has ever done anything impactful or significant in this world waiting on the approval of those who may be offended?" That is never been how rebellion works.

One of the most destructive things to tell a child is to" act normal" and "be like everyone else." One of the most damaging things to the ingenuity of a person is to instruct them to "get in where they fit in." I fully endorse the notion that you should dare to be different and refuse to be like everyone else. I believe that that kind of thinking is unhealthy for the human spirit. Everyone should be encouraged about their capability to accomplish amazing feats in their life. This belief is the foundation of developing positive self-image and establishing the habit of visualizing personal success. It is the key to buying into your future successes. Some may call it arrogance, but they do not know what it took for you to get to this place. Some may say you are self-centered, but they did not see the trials that you have had to overcome to be where you are. Though, you may not ultimately be where you want to be, in order to get there, you must start believing and visualizing yourself in that place. Remember that no one can ever want it for you any more than you want it for yourself.

A Rebellious Plan

November 22, 1963 will forever be a day that will live in infamy for everyone who was alive and all of us who love history. It was an afternoon that a generation would describe as one of the worst that they ever experienced. It was supposed to be a day of immense celebration for a historic visit to the Lone Star state and to its largest city, Dallas. This was the day that the 35th President of the United States was assassinated while riding in a convertible during a parade. This young president was one that was absolutely beloved by everyone who knew him. His name was John Fitzgerald Kennedy. The controversy that surrounded his death was astounding for many different reasons, but one of the major conspiracy theories was the "Magic Bullet."

A few hours after the murder of JFK and shooting of Governor John Connally, who was riding shotgun in that convertible, there was the arrest of Lee Harvey Oswald. Before Oswald ever saw the inside of a courtroom, he was gunned down by Jack Ruby, a Dallas businessman. Oswald was already convicted by all the media who covered the nationally-televised murder. Nonetheless, Oswald's death opened the door to several different theories that contended that Kennedy's assassination had more to do with some of his unpopular policy decisions. Some of those contentious policies were around civil rights for African-Americans and the Vietnam War. All of this led to conspiracy theorists suggesting that there was more than one person who shot Kennedy.

One of my favorite movies growing up was *JFK*, which starred Kevin Costner and instilled quite a bit of reasonable doubt in the idea that there was a single assassin. I can still see the diagram that showed the trajectory of the shots fired. With both President Kennedy and Governor Connally being struck by a single bullet was something that gave fuel to the whole mystery. They called it the magic bullet, because it was alleged that the single shot that went through the throat of Kennedy then paused, made a right turn in mid-air through the seat, and into Gov. Connally's shoulder and then his wrist. It is the most questioned theory that has been discussed and picked apart for years and proven again. It is a theory that will live forever.

The only reason that we are talking about a magic bullet is to say that regardless of this scenario, it does not exist for you. There will never be one thing that you can change or do or say or maintain that will provide you a shortcut toward success or a way for you to circumvent the process. Regardless of how many books you read that tell you that there are 10 steps or three keys or five secrets to unlocking some mythical transformation, it will not happen. There is no secret sauce or recipe that you can adopt today and see major growth and change tomorrow. I hate to be the one to burst your bubble and make the process a little less appealing, but I have never been one to sale anyone a dream. What you do have at your disposal is the knowledge that you always, always have the opportunity to adopt the necessary changes in your life. It may not be as simple as some people will make it seem, but the growth is everything that is advertised.

Previously, we discussed the "renewal of your mind," which is a fancy way to say that you must change what you think before you can change your behavior. Your pattern of behavior and the model it sets for your life can also be referred to as a paradigm. The idea of the paradigm is one that has been greatly over/misused particularly in progressive circles who consistently throw out the term, "paradigm shift." It is described as "a fundamental change in an individual's or society's view of how things work in the world," according to Dictionary.com. The thing that is often missed is that it is not something that is in any way topical. It will never be understood or interpreted by only looking, regardless of how intensely, at the surface level. So, when it comes to looking at the paradigm that governs your life, what makes you tick, the ideas that drive your ethics, it will require much more than a surface-level look at your life. This is where the idea of the magic bullet should die, because you cannot afford to believe there is some supernatural scheme that can help you get there. It is a tough journey. It is your journey.

In my primary school years, I was pretty amazing at math, and even would say I was advanced. This lasted until I got to high school in Mr. Van Sant's Geometry class where I no longer felt enthusiastic about the subject. There are a couple different reasons why I think this shift happened after I reflected on it a few years back. Firstly, I was tired of being the singular token Black kid in advanced classes filled with white counterparts. Those classes were culturally and socially insufficient for my growing consciousness and expanding racial pride. Secondly, I asked Mr. Van Sant and every math instructor afterward the same question to no avail, "Where would I ever use this in my adult life?" Over and over the question came back void and my interest diminished year after year. By the time I got to college, I was struggling immensely with college algebra and pre-calculus when just a few years earlier I was a top student. This experience taught me quite a bit about myself and gave me some invaluable insight about how to perceive life.

One of the most pressing lessons was the reality that I would always be a person who needed to know why I was doing something. It really put into focus all the times that I challenged a teacher or elder when something they told me never quite made sense. Over the years, I had gotten into so much trouble because I could never shut my mouth. I made a reputation for myself of always pushing my teachers to the brink of explosion, partly because I was inquisitive, and partially because I was mischievous. (Please, please, and please keep in mind that whatever you do there is such a thing as karma and it will find you. Elijah acts EXACTLY like I did as a kid. Thus, I fully expect that there will be many times in the future that will make me want to pull my hair out; I deserve it.) All of this led to the understanding that I need a purpose for everything that I do. It led me down this road of self-discovery toward what I wanted to do with my life. That no matter what it was, it had to have meaning and really matter to me. It was the start of a deepening understanding of what was necessary for me to be fulfilled in my everyday walk.

We can all remember a time when we were around family as young kids playing and having fun. We would be filled with joy and there would be plenty of smiles, laughter, and high spirits. That is until someone would bust into the room crying. One parent, or multiple, would start the line of questioning beginning with "What happened?" Through sobs and consoling, there would be a broken story that would involve two children. The other child would then be summoned into the room and give another version of the story where he explains the events but all happening by "accident." The hysterical child would often interrupt and say, "No, you did it on purpose." Then there would be an argument that ended with the parent making a judgment. After all this, the kids would be back in the next room playing as if nothing ever happened. The argument about whether it was done intentionally would be over and often forgotten already. I contend that when you are determining the direction of your life, you must learn to be navigate constructively while being purposeful with your every action.

One of my favorite quotes about purpose reads, "Efforts and courage are not enough without purpose and direction," which suffices to say that you must be intentional about everything. There is only so much that life will offer you without a plan or some intentional direction for where your life is headed. This is a reality that we all must come to grips with and speaks directly to the law of attraction. Buddha is noted as stating, "All that we are is a result of what we thought," which goes hand-in-hand with the premise behind the law, which is that you will bring into your life what your thought life focuses on. It says that if you think negatively then negativity will be headed your way, and the same goes for the consequence of positive thought.

This is similar to the psychological term of self-fulfilling prophecy that in its title insinuates that the outcome is self-determined or independently defined. The most robust definition that I found comes from Study.com and reads as follows:

> *When a person unknowingly causes a prediction to come true, due to the simple fact that he or she expects it to come true. In other words, an expectation about a subject, such as a person or event, can affect the behavior towards the subject, which causes the expectation to be realized.*

These theories were compiled into one of the best-selling books of this century, which sold 19 million copies, called *The Secret* written by Rhonda Byrne. In my opinion, it was an oversimplification of how the world operated and negated all the factors that determine growth. I felt it was a bolstering of the common adage (and greatest lie ever told) that you should "pull yourself up by your own bootstraps." That if you believe it will so.

This is to say that it was only the individual that made the difference for the direction of their life. It seemed unbelievably parochial and narrow-minded to me for quite some time. What I believe now has shifted considerably because your today, the 24-hours that we all have, cannot change your world. For example, if you bought a lotto ticket today and won $200 million dollars you still would not be able to claim your money or realize the considerable difference it will make in your life all in one day. So, one of the most critical realities that everyone must succumb to is that everything requires a process. I know this sounds somewhat redundant, but it is critical to being able to manage your struggle.

Subtract (-) Bias

It would be a reasonable assumption that those who have decided to subscribe to stereotypes and have developed certain prejudices against other people are consistently realizing those expectations. They bring into their lives whatever negative things their minds focus on. This is the worst thing that you can do regarding figuring out what it is that you must shed yourself of; things that do not progress your life. That goes for thinking, relationships, career decisions, and personal behavior. Everything that you dedicate time towards should be for the sake of future enrichment. One of the things that makes this possible is a sound understanding of your non-negotiables. What are those things that you cannot and will not compromise on? Where is that line in the sand? Who are the people who are essential to your future growth? How do you determine this code of ethics? These are crucial inquiries that must be reflected on.

Subtraction is an essential mathematical function necessary to complete a certain type of problem. It is the simplest way to decrease one figure from another. Subtraction is also a necessary step when considering the biases and relationships that you carry with you from year to year. One of the realities that I always share with young people is that, "the friends that you have today will not be your friends in 10 years."

Over the course of a few short years, there has been so much turnover in my life with people who I thought were going to be permanent. Just today, I told one of my students that she must develop an ability to discern who has her best interest for her future, and remove everyone else who does not; subtraction. It is no one's fault that people grow apart, it just happens naturally. Therefore, subtraction is a necessary part of everyone's life for math class and otherwise.

When we consider that the development of biases is as natural as breathing, we know that we must be willing to leave certain ones behind. Muhammad Ali proclaimed once, "A man who views the world the same at fifty as he did at twenty has wasted 30 years of his life." I believe we can all agree with this statement, and have no desire to be this person. We all want to grow and learn from the mistakes that we have made and undoubtedly will make in the future. It is vitally important to our impending success to consistently make wise decisions when it comes to personnel and actions after a learning experience (failure). We have a responsibility to ourselves to be prudent with these judgements, as they will shape the outcomes in our lives. These very outcomes will be the foundation that we must stand upon. They are the cornerstone of the life you envision for yourself. Each independent action or inaction can dramatically impact the direction of your life both positively and negatively.

In the words of Erykah Badu, "Evolving involves eliminating," which is exactly what must happen with your biases. When we consider what has happened in this political election season that culminated in the election of Donald Trump, we must know that the strength of biases is evident. These unchecked biases have led a large portion of our "inclusive" society toward deeply-rooted prejudices that manifested in a very ugly way.

We, as a country, have not evolved in the ways that we thought we did with the election of a Black president. The true ugliness that exists in the economically-underdeveloped, diversity-depraved regions of this country was astounding to everyone, even conservative pundits. It is even more obvious when you review any electorate map broken down by county. Any county with considerable diversity did not vote in favor of Trump while every county with 80+% Caucasian populations was solidly for "Making America Great Again."

A thorough examination of history offers insight into this idea that we must challenge and control other people. It can even be realized when we begin to unveil the biases we have for America. All the talk about "America is the greatest country in the world," is the great propaganda machine that we have in this country. It is this hardened bias that allows for a great portion of our society to view Colin Kaepernick's stance against oppression of Black people in this country as a slight. When people have more passion to demonize the protester than they do to address what is being protested, it says something about the strength of such biases. Our society, at large, has yet to grapple with how deeply rooted our biases, prejudices, and discriminatory habits have become. Thus, we cannot depend on society to teach us much of anything about tolerance or acceptance.

Privilege is loved by those who possess it and envied by those who do not. There is no reason to challenge its existence or question its inescapabilty. In these Divided States of America, we have equal issue with privilege, the financial ramifications of it, and class divisions as we do with race. For those who have this power, they wield it as they see fit, which has been consistent in their self-serving nature. This is the greatest challenge for the country that I see. Majority society's biases are very much so dependent on their privilege, but they must see the struggles of the common man from his perspective for anything to change.

If we can learn to look at biases as convenience, we can change the narrative in this country. So, the resistance to bias is truly a struggle against complacency. It is often the basis for what causes people to remain in place on the social or economic ladder. It requires an amazing amount of internal strength to be able to refuse to flow with the crowd. "Strength is the product of struggle, you must do what others don't to achieve what others won't," remarked Henry Rollins, the Aussie musician and actor. It cannot be captured more beautifully than this. Our inability to remain strong when common thought surrounds us is what inhibits our growth.

Remember when I wrote awhile back that nothing grows in comfort? That remains true. Growth is something that we all strive for, but we cannot fear struggle, strife, or strain that comes with it. Over the course of one's life, the greatest periods of evolution always come after some form of trial. For every mountain that we are forced to climb, we have a better view of what lies on the other side. Yet it is the process of climbing that develops the muscles we need to leave our biases, those comforts, behind permanently. Too much of anything is a bad thing, but when it comes to comfort and convenience it usually results in failure.

There are always varying degrees of success in the world, but one thing is always true for those who lack privilege...We must be willing to risk everything to attain success. You must be willing to leave what is safe behind to get what you want. We do not have the good fortune to be stagnant in life. For stagnation is akin to death for the unprivileged. Facing failure is something that we all must get accustomed to. If we are not willing to move aggressively in the direction of our dreams and challenge bias along the way, we will not be successful in any realm of our lives.

Biases, also known as convenience, also known as comfort,

also known as failure (if you refuse to be proactive), can be condemning unless you are willing to let things go. Albert Einstein said, "Once you stop learning, you start dying," which has and always will be true. Our lives depend on constant refinement that comes from continuous self-education. Similarly, the moment that we stop risking failure, the instant we accept our circumstances as permanent, and the second we decide to live without challenging our biases, our lives as rebels are terminated. The livelihood of the rebel is determined solely on how you embrace challenge, how you learn to handle stressors.

Add (+) Stress

Stress is something that we all have been conditioned to try to avoid. It has even made its way into doctor's offices across the nation as a contributor to health issues. Yet, stress is something that we all must deal with on a regular basis. Throughout our lives, we are all forced to push through whatever stressors exist and progress despite their existence. There is a new level of stress, or pressure, whenever we elevate ourselves to another level in life. There is a universal understanding that whenever you move up in the world, making more money or having more responsibility, it also adds more pressure to perform well.

In 2016, I am sure that everyone has heard an analogy or two about diamonds being made under pressure; this is true. But I always felt that it was more revealing that not the entire coal mine turned into diamond. Hundreds of feet below the surface and under tons of rock, there is always far more regular coals than diamonds. I think this is the simplest way to think about how your perception of adversity makes the difference to how you come out. I always say that you win or you learn, yet learning is the only way you ultimately win at life. Thus, failure, and the pressure that comes with it, can never truly harm you if you have the right mindset.

So, when we are discussing stress, we must be clear about what the perceived enemy is. Our enemy is not the obstacle itself, but fearing the change that comes from facing it. Because after we face a new challenge, we will always see change if we are honest with ourselves. It may not be immediate, it may need to be coupled with another experience for us to see the full value, but it always has an impact on our lives; for the positive if we allow it. So, when we talk about the stress that exists in our lives, we must learn to admit its intrinsic, enriching qualities.

These qualities are the basis for how stress can be used to fuel our growth. We have already confirmed that growth does not take place in comfort or convenience. Therefore, we must concede that struggle and challenge have a place in our lives. If we plan to defy the odds and resist stereotypical outcomes, we must conquer stress. We must make it our slave. We must imprison it until it has usefulness. If we cannot master this segmentation, we will constantly be overwhelmed by the unexpected. It will overpower our positive outlook on life and make us consider pessimism as a viable mode of operation. I have seen it happen far too many times in my career as an educator. They call it, "teacher burn-out." I call it, teacher psyched-out. They are slaves to the stressors of the educational atmosphere they are in. Nothing more or less.

"...There's nothing new under the sun/It's never what you do, but how it's done," proclaimed Nas on *No Idea's Original.* So, when someone comes to you to vent, you should not take on their concerns. You can never own their feelings about a situation or circumstance, which is to say that you cannot take on their stress or pessimistic perspective. One of the principal reasons there are not more rebels in the world today is because we have a lack of people who are willing to think for themselves. Have you ever heard the saying that misery loves company? Well, it is true. So, when you make the decision to change your outlook for the better, never be afraid to leave others behind. As you chart a course toward self-progression, there are people who will not want to see you improve.

Those people are what we call in the business...stepping stools; love them fiercely. They are amazingly important people to your life, because of what they represent in life. Whenever you have haters, it is an admission that you are doing something positive. Do not embrace these people because they are toxic, but appreciate them from a distance. There is so much to be learned from people who vehemently disagree with what you do or how you operate. But to be clear, you cannot afford to develop relationship with these kinds of people. Unless they are giving criticism to bring clarity to your perspective with hopes of making you a better person, they are toxic; stay away. Just because you rebuke relations with these people does not mean that you cannot glean something from their pushback. I digress.

It is important to believe that stress is for your betterment. People who frustrate you and/or challenge your perspectives are there to refine you. Perception is the basis for interpretation. If we continually perceive everything that is inconvenient as a threat, we will only growth as much as comfort allows. We have already debunked the myth that progression is found within coziness or safety. Thus, we must be willing to accept that stress is a natural part of growth, because by natural discomfort causes agitation, and agitation causes movement. That movement can only add new experiences to your life, if you are allowing them to drive you forward.

All great explorers, inventors, and innovators in history were willing to strike out on a path without the comfort of knowing what would be the outcome. They stared out into the great abyss and refused to believe in the vast nothingness. They saw an adventure waiting to happen. They perceived an opportunity to challenge the existing streams of thought. You must be willing to do the same for your life.

If we listen to the words of Nas, we know that there is nothing new in this world, and therefore we can learn from those who have come before us. We do not have to make the same mistakes as those who travelled the path already. We do not have to subject ourselves to the same stumbling blocks, because we have something many of our forebears did not: Google. During all this exploration, we have the good fortune to be born in a generation with unlimited access to guidance. So, whenever we are faced with a challenge, we can connect with as many people as we need to, as fast as we wish, gain as much clarity as we desire. This can never be discounted. This generation of rebels has far less to complain about and far more they can accomplish than their predecessors.

In Christianity, there is an age of accountability where it is said that God will hold people responsible for their ability or lack thereof to personally accept Jesus as their Savior. According to most religious scholars this is around the age of 12. Again, I do not expect others to subscribe to these beliefs, but think critically about that expectation it sets. Our souls are dependent on our ability to publically acknowledge and seek relationship with Jesus. When you apply this same principle to your life, you see things very differently. We must be willing to acknowledge opportunity in our lives and seek progression in every area of our personal development. This is the primary way we can truly guarantee our earthly salvation.

One of my favorite professors while at Morehouse was an adjunct professor, author, and orator named Dr. Daniel Black. Just recently, I came across these words from him: "We need to imagine ourselves as saviors…," which I believe says that we must see ourselves as the vehicles for progress. The status quo in our lives will only sustain us for so long before it will begin to hold us back. We cannot truly afford this.

So finally, stress should only drive you toward accomplishing your dreams. It should move you off your spot and demand something of you. If you allow the pressure of added stress to refine you, it will only make you a stronger person. Remember pressure creates diamonds while comfort produces nothing. Demand new, different, and challenging experiences for yourself. A little added stress makes all the difference to your future success, but there is only one thing that will make this process any easier.

Divide (÷) Purpose

Throughout this book, we have made it a point to speak on the development process to become a rebel in our world. There are several things that have been formulated to produce this prescription, but one of the most important ingredients has yet to be completely unpacked. We have spoken on a number of occasions about purpose and intentionality, but we must have comprehensive understanding of what that affords you.

We have also mentioned that rebels, in most cases, do not have an excess of privilege in this world. They often must be the ones who strike out on their own to make it happen. Please keep in mind that I do not make these connections to purpose with people who benefit from privilege, because their economic means, among other things, do not force them to deal with bias, stress, or purpose the same way as the rest of us. This is fundamentally important to remember, because we cannot afford to be disillusioned about who we are in this world. If there is one thing that social justice issues (law enforcement, police relations, environmental i.e. climate change, homophobia, xenophobia, misogyny, etc., etc. etc.) teaches us, it is that the haves do not care what impacts the have nots. (See Wall Street, Donald Trump and other billionaires, friends of Citizens United, and Dakota Access Pipeline owners' *modus operandi* for applicable examples.) The decision makers in our capitalist society are always thinking about what will allow them to accumulate more wealth regardless of the cost to the other 99% of our country. But the one thing that we can learn from these people is: You cannot afford to be without a defined purpose.

No matter what self-help book you pick up, they will tell you that you need to be intentional. That you must make up your mind about who you are to become. This level of intentionality is the foundation of what manifests itself as growth in your life. You cannot be living your purpose without first acknowledging that you made a choice that you are committed to. For example, I promised Rev. Collins that I would change the world of education and raise Elijah to become a good man. This book will prayerfully move me in the direction of doing both, because if I die today, I would have left him instructions. I am committed to this purpose for my life, as to ensure that my living was not in vein. It will never change though it may be refined or evolve. Every major action I take must be calculated and serve my greater purpose or I cannot engage in it.

When you have committed yourself to something much bigger than yourself, you must be willing to make sacrifices. The sacrifices will become more and more evident as you become more and more intentional in your everyday life. This shedding, so to speak, comes in the form of relationships or habits or even changing what we ingest (food or content). This level of intentionality is what will bring additional clarity in our lives to be able to focus on *our* purpose solely.

One of the most influential people I have had the fortune to come across through my association with Morehouse is Christian Perry. He was one of those big brothers who always told the unabashed truth and challenged everything about the way I perceived the world around me. It was not until I took a page out of his book and went without a phone for two months did I begin to understand his level of clarity. It was totally liberating and completely refreshing to be unplugged from society. I appreciated each moment for what it was and I have never been more fully present.

It is funny to think that years later, I am teaching students who cannot go 45 minutes without their phones or social media. Then it becomes clear that they are not being intentional about their consumption of information. They have spent their developmental years soaking up opinions from their peers in ways that do not force growth, because they are through mediums that are finite. This is the same reason why Elijah and I do not have game systems. There was something special about developing your own imagination and learning to make due without technology. It does something to your mind for the positive that technological advances have never been able to capture: it strengthens your independent thought muscles. These are the same muscles necessary to be intentional in a society of uncontrolled behaviors.

Intention is paramount to the execution of your purpose; this cannot be escaped or your purpose will go unfulfilled. Yet to draw motivation to execute your purpose, you must have a purpose that meets you exactly where your heart lies. I love art of all kinds and I will always love it. Once upon a time, I was damn good (if I do say so myself) at drawing, painting, and singing. Though I will always have deep affection for these talents, I would be doing myself and others a disservice by turning them into my life's work. Why? Because my passion for them will never carry me as far as my passion to impact the lives of young people. I had to make a conscious choice.

When we talk about purpose we can never ignore that it should be something that you are passionate about. Though my job can be emotionally draining at times, I am secure in the fact that my presence in my students' lives will make a difference. I have seen it firsthand and understand that it requires my presence regardless of any added frustrations. Want to know how you have identified a truly rebellious purpose? When you are doing something that ignites you to be selfless and it always feels seamless. At that point, your purpose will be transferable, thus allowing you to reach others, and it will be so wholly satisfying that it does not require second thought. It becomes instinctual.

I know I have talked before about the necessity to question everything and be critical as part of the prescription. That is still extremely important in your daily walk through life and helps with your intentionality, but when you live in your purpose that becomes fluid. Each and every day is about fine-tuning your behaviors and ensuring your navigational aspirations are efficiently being applied. Purpose is pervasive. Once you find it, it becomes the essence of who you are and no one can strip you of it. The gifts that we naturally possess and are passionate and disciplined enough to develop are what fuels our saunter aka swagger. The closer we come to succumbing to this reality as early as possible, the sooner we get a head start on creating the life we want. Purpose is the only comfort for the life of a rebel.

"We are all an amalgamation of our blessings and our purpose," remarked, the definition of an eclectic, passion-driven globetrotter, Jerald Cooper while attending a *My Brother's Keeper* event at the White House. If we are to believe that we are moving with purpose, we can never remove ourselves from those who have sacrificed for us to have this access. When establishing the groundwork for DNI, we had to accept that there were things totally out of our control. Some of those things worked in our favor as well. For us to have total ownership for our purpose, we must pay respect to the blessings or good fortune that we have been afforded.

When we connect with those who came before us, we can draw from their strength. This is our secret reserve that we can always come back to to refuel. There is always someone in the past who you can learn from, especially when you consider the ease and efficiency that we have in 21st century society. To think that our forebears did so much with so little, we can surely have equivalent ingenuity in these times. All this matters because there is no way to circumvent hurdles when striving to fulfill your purpose. Being able to reconnect with trailblazers in your chosen profession is instrumental to get through tough times. When you have dark days, they will make you question whether your purpose is correct. This is the appropriate time to reflect on what your predecessors did to overcome their moments of weakness or confusion.

A clearly-defined purpose coupled with intentionality and unwavering passion is the recipe to make your life as a rebel much simpler. As a rebel, you will already be faced with challenges that your peers will not. You will be forced to deal with pressures and doubts that will make the common man or woman cower. But not you.

You are someone who has made a conscious decision to impact the future of your family, of our society, and of our world starting with yourself. Never sell yourself short on what this decision means or how rare it has become to be diametrically different from your peers. If you add purpose unto such a clarion call, do not the possibilities seem endless? Without question! And I am a passionate possessor who takes full ownership of such bold action and will become someone in this world who will leave their mark. The history of our society is made of people who have lived purpose-filled lives and you can join them. Never forget that.

Multiply (×) Success

Success is a word overused and underappreciated in today's rhetoric-saturated world. This generation of young people are the first to collect participation trophies like championship banners. Thus, success has been watered down to mean far less than it did in the past. This watery version of what used to be reserved for the few has distorted our competitive culture of winners and losers. Frankly, I feel this is for the better as it fractures the indestructible façade of the American meritocracy. We need to see the chinks in the armor. We need to be able to see the humanity in the effort, even if that changes how people compete against one another.

The truth about rebels is that they are never in competition with anyone any way. They are competing against antiquated systems, unchallenged schools of thought, and personal accountability above all else. If they were not, they would be consumed with, what Jay-Z calls, the "shiny things" of this world. All of which are distractions from what is truly pertinent for your individual and our collective success. Christians commonly say that they are "in the world, not of it," which is to say that subscription to the standards of our society are not required to sustain yourself.

The primary function of the rebel is to learn to interpret the environment around them, and be critical of it enough to challenge it to better itself. That has always been the place of the rebel in this world and it will continue to be their space. But the distortion between what has always made the rebel's presence so powerful and universal and what society calls a rebel has always been polar opposites. It does not serve any society's agenda to celebrate those who buck the system and make substantive change. If it did there would be far more training in school that spoke to social and economic uplift tailor-made to each student. It is much better to have a heavy majority of sheep in our society than to have a preponderance of wolves. The rich do not get richer that way. When we address what success looks like, we must be willing to accept that the definition is fluid. Thus, we will take the position of what success does not look like for the rebel.

We have a simple equation that we have laid out: Subtract bias, add stress, divide that by purpose, and you will multiply success. This simple formula in reverse should expose the dangers of following what others do in our society. If you think critically about it for a moment, you will also see the allure that it offers as well. Applying this equation to your life will allow for the floodgates of achievement to be unlocked and never to be resealed. But first things first, we must destroy the glamor that exists with being just like everyone else.

Have you ever imagined or fallen victim to living in a purposeless reality? One where you move aimlessly through life and act without motive? Without hope? If you do not actively work to determine your passion and find your purpose in life, you are living to survive, not to thrive. You would be living a life that is bland, odorless and colorless, which you will constantly seek small thrills to give your life a sense of meaning.

This is the reality for so many people in this world who have become so discontent that they refuse to fight for their rightful place in it. They accept whatever comes as a precondition to circumstance. These people refuse to get their hopes too high, because disappointment has always followed elevated expectations. Inaction is the order of the day as they cannot be moved by the frustrations of life to activate themselves. They have no coping mechanism for their pain because they have nothing constructive that they can put their dissatisfaction toward; remember hurt people hurt people. Passion only exists when they are serving self and succumb to their carnal desires. This is a purposeless life; this is an aimless quest for the next high. Wandering through life's ups and downs searching for constant relief outside of themselves. Riddle me this: Can you afford to live absent purpose? *insert reflection here*

What if you only did what was simple and unchallenging? What if whenever you were faced with an obstacle you retreated? What if fear ruled your life? What if it stopped you from changing your routine? When you never learn to deal with stress and what causes it, you will always live on the defensive. Life will always be coming at you faster than you can seemingly protect yourself. Therefore, you are trapped in perpetual chaos with no ability to escape its clutches. The only safety available will be isolation, the only peace you will find will be with idleness.

This is the story that people who tell themselves cannot accept the challenges that life offers us all. They struggle immensely with motivation and remain frustrated with the cards that life has dealt them. Their first instinct is to shrink and hope to go unnoticed as it is easier to run from tension then to confront it. The frustrations of life are too much to handle and so they are always looking for a sedative, something to numb themselves with. They solely pursue cushy lives while managing simple tasks to barely keep their heads above water. There is no growth or opportunity to build with other people; relationship causes conflict. There is limited to no new experiences as they care more for their routine then to challenge their status quo. Fantasy consumes these people's lives because reality is too taxing to come to grips with. They reject living within our society outside of enough to cover their basic needs. Riddle me this: Are you willing to lead a life without a willingness and ability to cope with stress? *insert reflection here*

What would your life resemble if you never moved from your comfort zone? How would it feel to only allowed convenience to dictate your actions? What if that convenience determined where you went? How you perceived others? What if your biases impacted your relationships with everyone outside of your race? Outside of your gender? Sexual orientation? Socioeconomic status? These are the thought processes of a great portion of our society, yet does not acknowledge the ever-changing world around us.

Without a healthy ability to seek understanding of those different than yourself, you always stay in "comfortable" situations with "suitable" people; echo chambers. You never move beyond the perceptions that you have and become prisoner to the thinking of the environment. Critical thought is unimportant and discouraged in these places, which makes it that much easier to hide the fact that you cannot think for self. Every bias you have lives as an extension of what you heard from a louder (and perceived stronger) voice than your own. There is no critical thought or intellectual conversation based on facts, but rather raw, unchecked emotion. Regurgitation is the standard and independent thought is damn-near forbidden. Newness is an assault to the way things have always been. New perspectives are stamped out quickly without complete understanding. The individual matters little in this world. The individual is a pawn just like everyone else, thus your mind can scarcely produce anything worthwhile. And by chance it does too often, you will be considered a pariah. You will be rejected. You will be disconnected from the body. Cast out. Riddle me this: Are you prepared to create a life of a follower without a voice of your own subservient to the biases of the masses?

Whether it is purpose or stress or bias that holds you back, we should be able to all agree that there is something deeply flawed in surrendering to them. It would be an unreasonable expectation to believe that everyone in the world has what it takes to become a rebel. There are some people who will read this book at 17 and not realize change until 28; that is a reality.

Everyone will move at their own pace which usually is dictated by circumstance. When you want to succeed as bad as you want food, you will make a change. When your hunger for better conditions is stronger than your need for convenience than you will become laser-focused. When your desire to change your outcome conquers your lack of discipline or procrastination than sleep will no longer matter. Unfortunately for most of us, we must have our backs against the wall to make the proper decision to initiate wholesale improvement in our lives. Comfort is intoxicating and its magnetism is stronger than we think, which is what gives it permanence in our lives. Nonetheless, we must constantly embrace the ideals of a rebel. We must be willing to fight back against the status quo's existence in our lives personally, professionally, and publically.

For those who are dedicated to dissention, amped for altercation, and calling for controversy, this book may not be what you were looking for. For those of us who are more concerned with what are the stages to critical actualization of their purpose, you should have found this reading enlightening. You can find success in your ability to adopt this doctrine in your everyday life. Success for you is possible.

Rebellion is something in today's world that begins with the individual willing to make significant change in his or her life. Then finding others who subscribe to a similar school of thought that are equally dissatisfied with the status quo. That union centered around a shared institutional purpose is how movements are ushered into existence. And with that in mind, I would like to cordially invite you to rebel. Join us on this side... Your inner rebel will thank you later.

The Start

Carlton Robert Collins is a consultant, edupreneur, facilitator, speaker, and writer with over a decade of experience in education ranging from recruitment of minority educators nationwide, strategic development for clientele as well as college placement and career exploration for scholars throughout Greater Cincinnati and Metro Atlanta. Currently, Collins operates EDUC8theWORLD, an educational consultancy that has national and regional clientele focused on driving innovative cultural engagement solutions and youth development for youth and young adults. He is a 2011 graduate of Morehouse College with a Bachelor's in History and currently is at the University of Cincinnati in the M.A. Instructional Design & Technology program. He has served on numerous boards and aided in numerous initiatives including Secretary of Morehouse College National Alumni Association ('12-'14). His intergenerational pedagogy is heavily influenced by the work of Paulo Freire, Marian Wright Edelman, James Baldwin, and many other trailblazers. Collins is the proud father of one son, Elijah Mitchell, and committed husband to his wife and business partner Rosalyn living in his hometown of Cincinnati, OH.